SPOUSE HUNTING:

USING THE RULES OF REAL ESTATE TO FIND THE LOVE OF YOUR LIFE

Brian Belefant, Licensed Oregon Broker

ISBN: 9780962955501

Table of Contents

Getting Started

Listing

Purchasing

Making and Accepting Offers

Negotiating

Closing

Happily Ever After

Dedication

The part of the book about real estate is lovingly dedicated to my children because let's be honest, no thing, no person, no pet (not even Milo, the Best Puppy Ever™) means as much to me as they do.

Everything I do, everything I am, is for them and because of them.

The part of the book about finding a partner is dedicated to my ex-wife. She taught me everything I know about what a good partnership isn't.

How to Read This Book

I set out to write a book and wouldn't you know it? It turned into two. The first book is an outline of the 99 rules of real estate as I know them — 99 things you should know and do when you're buying and/or selling a home.

The second book is where it gets neat. Almost every single rule of real estate can be applied to buying and/or selling a partner.

Wait, that's not what I meant. I meant "can be applied to finding a partner and/or presenting yourself as someone that someone would want to be a partner with."

Glad I caught that before we printed this thing.

Anyway. I put the two books into one, with the real estate rule on the left; the finding-a-partner analog on the right. If I get all explainy and a rule goes on for more than a page, it'll continue after you turn the page on the same side — real estate on the left, true love on the right. With a little arrow at the bottom to help guide you.

Got it? Good. Let's get started.

Getting Started

Rule #1
Gird Your Loins

Buying or selling a home can be a long, frustrating, painful process. Especially buying.

And really, it's supposed to be. After all, you're looking for THE ONE. You don't want just any home. You want your home. Something special.

You're going to have to kiss a lot of frogs.

If you actually find a frog that turns out to be a less frog-like frog, a crane might swoop down and gobble up the frog. The frog might meet another princess. Or more likely, another frog. Hell, the frog might spontaneously explode.

Too much metaphor. But you know what I mean.

The best thing you can do is prepare yourself for a long,

⇩

Finding a partner can be a long, frustrating, painful process.

And even more than finding a house, it's supposed to be. After all, you're looking for THE ONE. The person you plan to spend the rest of your life with. You don't want just any partner. You want your special someone.

You're going to have to kiss a lot of frogs.

Trust that your person is out there. And if you follow all the steps, eventually you'll find them.*

Until you find them, keep telling yourself: It's meant to be hard. Because you don't want just anybody. You want someone special.

The harder it is to find that person, the more you'll appreciate them when you do. Everybody can't be special. More important, everybody shouldn't be.

Go watch *The Incredibles* again. It's an amazing movie with a profound message: Special is, well, special.

---

* My mother was an English professor, so I was trained never to use the third person plural pronoun as the object in a sentence like this, but it's even more awkward to constantly say him/her or his/her, so there you go. Sorry, Mom. And yes, I split an infinitive. Steven Pinker says it's okay.

dispiriting, frustrating, stupid slog. And the best way to prepare yourself is to have three things: clarity, focus, and a sense of humor.

This book will help you have all three.

Clarity comes first. It's the stuff in the first section (Rules #1 through #16).

Focus comes from the process — the steps you take, one at a time, to accomplish your goal (Rules #17 through #99).

And a sense of humor comes from your father. Or maybe alcohol.

Hell, I don't know where a sense of humor comes from. All I know is that it helps to have one. If you follow all the steps and laugh along the way, it's still likely to be painful and stupid, but it'll be a lot more fun.

Rule #2
Don't Wing It

Playing the Powerball is a shitty strategy for getting rich. And wandering into open houses is a shitty strategy for finding a home.

Don't get me wrong. It could happen. I'm just saying don't count on it. When you really want something, you have to make a plan.

Here's the thing about plans, though. They don't have to be super detailed. You don't need charts and graphs, and you sure as hell don't need those things they show in movies about serial killers, with the yarn connecting newspaper clippings and photos all taped to the wall. What is that shit anyway? Does that even make sense?

I'm going to give you a much simpler way to think of a plan. Ready? It's three things.

Direction. This is where you want to be. True love looks awesome in the movies, but in real life it's hard. Think it through.

⇩

Just like playing the Powerball is a shitty strategy for getting rich and wandering into open houses is a shitty strategy for finding a home, going to singles bars is a shitty strategy for finding love.

I mean, yeah, it could happen. I'm just saying don't count on it. When you really want something — whether it's a house or true love — you have to make a plan.

On the other side — the real estate side — I talked about it as three things: where you want to be, where you are, and a plan to get there. I'm going to put it another way here. Ready?

Position. Same thing as "Where are you now?" Have you unpacked your baggage from that heinous divorce? Are you ready to actually open yourself up to another person? Is there anything that will keep you from being able to make that kind of commitment? Like, oh I don't know, are you already in a relationship?

Picture yourself down the road — way down the road. (Rule #4 will help.) If you're not absolutely certain that a serious relationship is

Number One. The first thing you need is a really clear picture of what you want. The clearer the better. If you know exactly what you're looking for, you're going to recognize it when it shows up. And it will because the second thing you need is…

Number Two. A plan to get there. And then there's…

Number Three. An honest understanding of where you are now.

Let me put it another way.

If you want to get to the corner of 52nd and Madison and you're at the corner of 41st and Lexington, you know you have to go eleven blocks uptown and one block crosstown.

Clear picture of where you want to be = 52nd and Madison.

Plan to get there = go uptown for eleven blocks and then go crosstown for one.

Honest understanding of where you are = 41st and Lexington.

If you get to 51st and Madison and you're like, "You know

what you want, put this book down and go find something else to do.

I'm serious. If you aren't absolutely clear about where you want to go, you might get where you're heading, but you probably won't be happy when you arrive.

Think of it this way. If you want to meet a woman who's one in a million and you haven't clarified who she is and what your relationship is like, you better be prepared to meet a million women.

That means ten women a day for 100,000 days. (Obviously, this goes for men, too.)

Speed. When you know where you are and where you want to be, all you have to do is go. One step at a time. And that's exactly what the rest of this book is. The steps. One at a time.

🏠

what? Nah. I'd rather be at 82nd and Third," you really didn't have a clear picture of where you were going, did you?

And if you go 34 blocks downtown and two blocks crosstown, you're not actually following the plan. And if you're actually starting out in Cleveland, you're not doing an honest appraisal of where you are.

Get this stuff straight. I'll help. Starting with Where You Are.

Let's go to the next rule.

Spouse Hunting: Using The Rules Of Real Estate To Find The Love Of Your Life

Rule #3
Commit to Committing

This is going to sound really simple, but that's because it is. If you want to buy a house, you have to want to buy a house. And if you want to sell a house, you have to want to sell a house.

Think of it this way: Most people would love to have a million bucks. But what do they do? Do they work on getting a million bucks? Or do they hang out on the sofa with their hands down the front of their pants, watching reruns of *Family Guy*?

Committing to committing means getting a home is important. Important enough that you're going to pursue that goal above other goals.

Way more important than letting inertia keep things the way they are.

If you want a relationship, you have to want to want a relationship. It has to be important. More than important, it has to be critical.

And this requires clarity. Do you want to find The One or do you want to get laid? Do you just want to hang out with friends? Do you want to use dating sites as a way to connect to potential clients? (Don't laugh. I know people who do this.) Do you just want to be left alone?

Think long and hard and if you decide that yes, you want a partner, commit to finding a partner.

Once you do, think about heroes in movies. They have Single-Minded Determination. When you watch heroes in movies, they don't stop chasing the bad guy to have a sandwich. In fact, try to find a scene in any movie about a hero trying to accomplish something in which that person eats, sleeps, or uses the bathroom. You're rarely going to find one. A hero is constantly in pursuit of a goal. They don't

make movies about people doing their laundry, hanging out in the video arcade, or walking their dogs. I mean, yeah, they do. But when they do it's almost always as a way to make the point that they're not actively pursuing the thing they want.

Yeah, you have a life. You have to go to work, clean the house, pick up the kids, make dinner, all those things. So you can't live like a hero in a movie. That's okay. Movies last 90 minutes. You get more time.

Just don't waste the time you have.

Rule #4
Get Pre-approved

You may think you're ready. But are you?

No really. Are you?

Guess what. It's not entirely up to you to answer that question.

If you want to buy a house, you need to have a loan.* Which means you need to get a lender to check out your income, your debt, and your credit score and come to the conclusion that you're the kind of person they can trust to repay a mortgage. (Your Position, from way back in Rule #2.)

Finding a lender is easy. Start with your bank. Go in and tell them what you're thinking. Be honest about your finances. They'll let you know whether you qualify and if you don't, what you need to do.

* Unless you're rich. But you're not.

When it comes to finding love, there's no bank or credit union or mortgage broker to officially proclaim that you're ready emotionally, psychologically, and yeah, financially to move forward. But you have friends, right? Family? Maybe a therapist?

Tell them what you're thinking: That you think you're ready to commit to a long-term relationship.

Then shut up and listen.

And listen carefully. You know how friends are. They like you. They don't want to hurt your feelings.

They might agree. Or they might tell you that there's still some work you need to do — maybe you need to repair your "credit score."

If that's the case, do the work. Get your life in order. And when you're ready, ask them again.

One important point, and this goes for whether it's love or a home you want: Make sure you're looking for a pre-approval from someone who understands you and your situation. A lot of banks, for

Spouse Hunting: Using The Rules Of Real Estate To Find The Love Of Your Life

instance, aren't comfortable evaluating someone who's self-employed. (A good realtor — like me, for instance — will introduce you to lenders who are good at evaluating people in situations like yours and can often see that you're ready when other, more conservative institutions expect nothing but disaster. I can't help you with the friends and family thing, though.)

This is important. If you try a bunch of different places and you keep hearing the same thing — that you're not ready to make a commitment — take a good, hard look at yourself.

They probably know. Also — and I realize this is hard to accept — they're telling you for your own good.

Rule #5
Make a List

You know how the Supreme Court defines porn, right? They know it when they see it.

That may work when you're doing something with no serious repercussions, like, oh, I don't know, codifying laws that affect millions of people, but it simply doesn't fly when you're looking for a house.

You need to know what things you're looking for. And you need to be clear with yourself about how important each of those things is.

Most clients I work with start out with a vague idea of what they want, so the first thing we do is fill out a worksheet that makes them clarify the deal breakers, the things they'd like but might be willing to give up, and the things they're attracted to.

It's probably obvious how each of the sections works, but in case it isn't...

When I work with real estate clients looking to buy a house, I very strongly recommend that they make a list. I also very strongly recommend that they break the list down into three sections: Deal Breakers, Must Have A Compensating Reason, and What You're Attracted To. Hey, guess what! It's exactly the same with looking for a partner!

• Deal breakers. You may decide that religion is important. Or that your partner has to be employed. (This comes from my friend Abby, who told me about the list thing in the first place. She told me how it had worked for her, but also gave me a warning: "Make sure you include everything in the list." She found her person, but she'd forgotten to put Employed. The guy she found was everything she was looking for, but also couldn't get a job.)

• Must have a compensating reason. In my list of things I'm

- Deal breakers. If it isn't there, you move on. If you can't live without three bedrooms, it doesn't matter how swell that two-bedroom house is, you shouldn't buy it.

- Must have a compensating reason. This is stuff that's super important, but you'd consider giving up if there were a good reason. Let's say you reallllllllllly want a big front yard. Okay. Would you consider a house with a small front yard if it happens to be across the street from a park?

- What You're attracted to. What turns your head. You may happen to love the look of industrial lofts, but with two kids, a dog, and at least seven projects you're working on at any one time, you'd be an idiot to think you could actually live in one. But hey, maybe there's something about the look of a loft that you can get in a more conventional house.

looking for in a woman, one of my Must Have A Compensating Reason items is that she has to have kids. If she doesn't have kids, I need to know that she understands what it means to have kids and how important my kids are to me. So maybe she's a teacher. Or she has a really close family with nieces and nephews.

I know what you're thinking. You're thinking, Brian, why don't you just make Must Understand How Important My Kids Are To Me one of the Deal Breakers?

Shut up.

Seriously, the difference between these two sections — Deal Breakers and Must Have A Compensating Reason — is about degree. Deal Breakers either are or aren't. If a person doesn't have the thing, that's it. Move on.

With stuff in the Must Have A Compensating Reason section, I like to think of them on a scale of one to five. The more it's missing, the better the compensating reason needs to be.

- What You're attracted to. I love the look of women who do yoga. The way they hold themselves? Wow. But do I do yoga myself? Nope. That's why I need this section. What it does is (hopefully) keep you from falling in love with someone who's not right for you. Or maybe makes you realize that you should take up yoga.

This list thing works, and I'm not just saying this because Abby met that unemployed guy. If you want to get all spiritual, the universe manifests what you put out there. And maybe it does. Or maybe it's just that if you consciously decide what it is you want, you'll recognize it when it shows up.

Also, and this is important, you're going to meet people who meet all your criteria and still don't do it. That's when you go back to the list and make revisions.

"Really," you say? "You can do that?"

Yep. Unless you write it in stone, which you didn't.

In real estate there's a concept of Highest and Best Use. What that means is that the features and characteristics of a property are maximized. You want to find the partner who will give you your highest and best use, and vice versa. So tweak that list as necessary.

And that brings me to…

'

Remember how I said way back in the very beginning that this is going to be a long, agonizing process? This is why. The important word there is "process." Try, evaluate, change. That's a process.

Rule #6
Buying and Selling Are Two Separate Transactions

Looking for a new home is what we call Buying. But if you're also selling the home you're in, you're Listing. (This doesn't hold if you're renting or couch surfing or living with your parents, and if one of those is the situation you're in, you probably don't need to worry about this bit.)

If you're doing both buying and selling, it's important to structure the transactions so that one is what we call Contingent on the other. What that means is one of two things: Either the purchase can't be completed unless and until you've sold the home you currently own. Or the home you're listing can't be sold unless and until you've found another home to buy.

Which one, you ask? That depends on whether you're in a buyer's or seller's market, the features and condition of the home you're selling, and how picky you are about the home you're looking

Think of looking for a new partner as Buying. Think of the partner looking for you as your Listing. You're putting yourself on the market and hoping to find the most qualified buyer.

The important part here is to recognize that while you're buying, you're also selling. And that both of these transactions will work out best if you're on the same timeline, with the same property.

I'm going to go into the buying side first because I operate on the presumption that you want to partner with someone who wants to partner with you. So the first step is to find the pool of likely partners. After that, I'll get into the best ways to market to that pool so that you create a listing that will attract the most qualified buyers.

for. A good realtor (me, for instance) can help you figure out which one you want to do.

But remember, you want to do one. If you don't, you may find yourself owning two homes at the same time. Which can be awkward. Not to mention expensive.

Rule #7
Turn That List Inside Out

You made your list, right?

The list.

The list from the section before last.

Jesus, am I writing English here? Didn't I just go on in Rule #3 about how you have to commit to committing? I know I did. And I know you were nodding along as you read it.

And then in Rule #5, what did I say? I said make a list.

Go make your goddamn list.

It doesn't have to be your final list. In fact, it probably isn't. As you see stuff and think of stuff, you'll modify it. But you can't modify something that you don't have.

Make the list. I'll be here when you get back.

Christ, you people…

You made your list, right?

Now think about the person who's out there looking for you.

Start by taking the list you made in Rule #5 and ask yourself honestly if you have those same characteristics. If you're looking for someone healthy, are you healthy? If not, what would make you appealing to someone who pursues a healthy lifestyle?

I'm not saying you have to have all of the characteristics you're looking for in a partner, but you have to face the fact that if you don't, you better have a compelling reason for them to want to be with you.

You could be a project.

You could be a moderating force.

You could have so much of something else they're looking for that they'll overlook a deficiency in one category in order to be with you. Like money. Money works.

Just don't delude yourself, that's all I'm saying.

Okay. You made your list?

Good. Now go make two more. You made the list of what you're looking for in a home. The next one is what the person selling the home you want is looking for in you.

This may not be important. In some markets, more homes are being sold than there are buyers for them and sellers are grateful to have any offer come in.

But in others (Portland, for example) there are more buyers than there are houses for them to buy, so the sellers get to choose from among several suitors. I'll get into making an offer later, but at this point, it's important to think about what those sellers are looking for in a buyer and yeah, money is usually the biggest factor. But there are other things as well and sometimes money isn't really at the top.

Who are you?

What do you do for a living?

What do you do for fun?

Once you have the list, give it a good hard look. Is there anything you want to change? If there is, now is the time to do it. Not only because you'll be more likely to attract someone who shares your values, but because you'll actually be more true to your values.

What do you believe? Hate? Love?

Listing

Rule #8
Make Necessary Repairs

Now that you've gone through your house and make that second list, you've been reminded of all the things that need fixing.

Fix them.

If your house has a broken window, fix it. If the carpet is coming up, tack it down.

Two reasons. The first is that when people see little problems, they imagine big problems. (And they're usually right, but I'll get into disclosure and inspection and appraisal and repair addendums and all that later.)

The second is that until you sell the place, you live in it. There's no telling how long it'll take to sell, so doesn't it make sense to make your life more comfortable until it does?

It does. Take care of your shit.

Could you stand to drop 15 pounds? I know I could.

Do you drink a little more wine, smoke a little more weed than you think you should?

I'm not saying you need to convert yourself into something you aren't. I actually believe the opposite. You should be the absolute truest version of yourself that you can be.

Don't look for some objective criteria that you need to meet. Look for the things that are inconsistent with who you see yourself to be — and who you want others to see you as. (Hot tip: they're the same.)

For me, one of the things I care about most is integrity. But integrity is hard, especially when you're dealing with others who don't live by the same standards.

I was working with a client and we simply weren't seeing eye to eye. I did my best, but they weren't satisfied. Once we were done, I had a very difficult conversation with the client. I hated having it, but

.

I needed to. They told me all (well, some) of the ways that I didn't deliver what they expected. I'd already been paid, so I took out my checkbook and refunded them my entire fee.

I didn't have the money. At the time I was living on fumes and it hurt so very much to know that I might end up eating cat food and sleeping under a bridge, but I had made the decision that the next — final — partner in my life needed to be principled and so integrity absolutely had to be a deal breaker for myself in every aspect of my own life.

I overreacted. I know this now. I should have tried to work out a compromise where they felt as if they'd gotten their money's worth for the work I'd done. But at the time I had just extricated myself from a relationship with someone whose moral compass pointed to an entirely different north than mine. I was determined to live with integrity and I was willing to sacrifice what little financial security I had in order to do it.

I'm not going to tell you that there's a happy ending here. I'm still not out of the woods financially and it's still too early to tell you that I've found the love of my life. But you know what? I'm glad I did what I did. At least now when I have trouble sleeping, it's because things are hard, not because I've compromised my values.

I'm true to myself.

Rule #9
The Market Sets the Value

Value and price are not necessarily the same, but price is the closest thing we have to correlate with value, so when it comes to stuff like senators and flat-screen TVs, we use money to talk about what a thing is worth.

Price is really just a form of information. An equivalentator. It tells you how many cashmere sweaters it takes to get a garden shed, for instance.

With real estate, when you think in terms of equivalence, it's easy to do an idiot check on the listing price of a property. If you (or Zillow or your realtor) come up with a "value" of $580,000, take a look at other houses you can get for $580,000. Does your house stack up?

Speaking of Zillow, the easiest (and laziest) way to determine the market value of a property is to rely on someone else. Zillow,

Call me idealistic, but I don't believe that when it comes to love, your market value has anything to do with money. Or much to do with money, anyway.

When it comes to love, what your market value has to do with is intangible.

You can't put a number on hard work, loyalty, sense of humor, compassion, sense of adventure, or any of the other things that make you valuable to a potential partner. But what you can do is figure out what you want a partner to value in you and how important you want that to be.

This is more important than I'm making it sound.

About 20 years ago, I was super healthy. I ran seven miles a day. I had glorious hair down to my shoulders. I had a successful career in a sexy industry and I was making so much money that I had a hard time spending it all.

⬇

Redfin, Trulia, Realty.com, and a bunch of other sites have algorithms that will spit out what they say a place is worth. The thing about these sites is that they can't possibly know your home personally. And all they know about your neighborhood is what can be converted into digital information. That's why they're not only often way off from reality, they're way off from each other.

Any decent real estate professional will run what's called comps. Comparative sales. They'll mark out the boundaries of your neighborhood and figure out what properties have the same or similar bedrooms, bathrooms, square footage, and lot size sold for. The average is your comp.

Sometimes it's accurate. Often it's not.

A better real estate agent is either familiar with your neighborhood or willing to learn about it. They'll run the numbers a bunch of ways to figure out how to price it in the market —not just compared to your neighborhood, but also compared to other, similar

⇩

I was swept off my feet by one of the many women I'd swept off of theirs. She bought what I was selling because what I was selling was superficial. I bought what she was selling because what she was selling was equally superficial.

It's not that I didn't have principles, but my "market value" was based on the hair, the body, the career, and the money. So the "buyers" I attracted were the ones who valued things like my 1955 Mercedes convertible more than my work ethic.

I allowed myself to consider factors like a sense of humor and pretty (which, I'm not going to lie, are important to me) over factors like integrity, willingness to see something through, and empathy (which if I were to actually think about it, would have been way more important to me).

I did the equivalent of letting Zillow tell me what I should be selling for. And I bought from the available properties that happened to be on the market at the time.

⬇

neighborhoods. The agent will also get to know your house, and will look for those special things in both the house and the neighborhood that buyers can fall in love with. That tree in the back yard where a kid could have a tree house. The fact that one of the neighbors likes to decorate the crap out of his house for Halloween. And they'll compare your house to others that are currently for sale because that's exactly what buyers will be doing.

If you're looking for a quick sale, you don't need to bother with this stuff. A bunch of services have sprung up that will hand you a wad of cash and have you out of your home by the weekend. Just remember that in exchange for convenience and time, you're giving up money. A lot of money. They'll buy your house for cheap and then do everything they can to maximize what they get for it when they turn around and sell it to someone else. For what it's "worth."

The bottom line is, it doesn't matter what somebody says your house is worth unless they're ready to write up a contract for that number. Otherwise, it's just an opinion.

When the transaction you get into is based on the superficial stuff, trust me, your relationship will be too. The woman I married couldn't muster any interest when I started losing my hair and I cut back on exercise in order to try and make a living when work started to dry up. And when my business manager embezzled pretty much everything — and I had to sell my house to pay off the debts she'd racked up for me — instead of support from my wife, what I got was expressions of disappointment.

To be fair, my wife felt betrayed. Which turned into resentment. Which turned into helping herself to what was left of my savings to hire lawyers to extract what she felt entitled to from me.

I write this as a cautionary tale. Be very clear what you're selling and what it's worth. Because sooner or later you will attract a buyer and you better be damn sure it's the right one.

Rule #10
Don't Fix Up in Order to Sell

In Rule #8 I said fix. Not renovate.

One of the biggest mistakes I see people make is renovating a bathroom or adding a bedroom in order to sell.

Don't. Do. It.

It's a mistake for two reasons.

The first is that you'll never recoup your investment. Yes, even if you do the work yourself. I've seen studies that conclude that the most beneficial improvement you can make to a home is to renovate a bathroom and that if you do, you can expect to get a 40% return on your investment.

In other words, if you spend $30,000 fixing up a bathroom, it'll add $18,000 to the value of your house.

But there's a bigger reason. What the hell are you thinking?

Renovating a bathroom doesn't just cost money. It takes time. It

People do the same thing when it comes to love. They start going to the gym. They take classes in Polish cinema. They volunteer at the food bank.

Those are awesome things to do, but if you're doing them to make yourself more appealing to the person you want to meet, I say don't bother.

You're being deceptive. You're selling a falsehood. And once you've nabbed that partner, how quickly are those pounds going to come back? How many more Krzysztof Kieslowski films are you going to sit through? Are the homeless people going to have to go back to dumpster diving?

Do those things. Especially the course in Polish cinema because seriously, Krzysztof Kieslowski was a fucking god. But do them because you want to be a better person. Not because you want to fool someone into believing you're a better person.

creates stress and causes a lot of inconvenience. If you're going to go through all that, wouldn't you want to actually enjoy the goddamn bathroom?

Seriously. I'm not saying don't fix up the house. But fix it up for yourself, not for the people you hope are going to buy it.

⇩

Think of it this way. Is the person you want to meet someone who pretends to be amazing? Wouldn't you be a lot happier meeting someone who actually is amazing?

Rule #11

Know the Market so You Can Set Reasonable Expectations

The market determines value. We know that because I just said so in Rule #9. So if you want to know the value of something, you kinda have to know the market it's being sold and bought in.

But it gets more complicated. There's the market and then there's the market. And then there's the market.

What I mean by that is there's the national housing market, which is what they talk about on CNN. That's where they use terms like "housing starts" and "interest rates" and basically what you can learn from that is how things are kind of going in a general way all over the country.

This stuff's important because when interest rates are lower, houses are cheaper. Not cheaper meaning a $340,000 house is now $320,000, but since the vast majority of Americans buy houses on

$$\Downarrow$$

You can't use money to talk about love (you're not supposed to, anyway), but it's the market that determines value, so what does that mean, exactly?

What that means is — putting it in crass commercial terms — it comes down to supply and demand. Are there more potential partners looking for someone like you or are you competing with a lot of other people for attention?

So how do you determine what kind of a market you're in?

Look around. Do some research. Do you see more unaccompanied men or women? Are there more profiles for men or women on dating sites? Are there more total profiles? Are hookup sites doing relatively better than relationship sites?

If you're competing in the LGBTQ arena, it gets a little harder. You can't use demographics like gender to calculate demand and supply. But at the same time, demand is essentially the same as

credit, lower interest rates mean less interest you have to pay in order to buy the house.

Let's say interest rates drop from 5% to 4.5%. That $340,000 house goes from having a payment of $1,642/month to $1,550/month. Ish.

See? Cheaper.

After the national housing market, there's the regional market. That's what's going on in your area.

Did your city just pass a law making it illegal to restrict housing to single family residences? And another one requiring landlords to pay tenants thousands of dollars when they ask them to move out? Mine did. Those things are going to affect home prices here, but if you live in Cleveland, meh.

And then, after the regional market, there's the neighborhood.

Lots of things can affect the price of homes in a neighborhood and some of them have catchy names, like The Starbucks Effect.

supply. What you can do is see how prevalent your particular preference is relative to the general population. In Portland, LGBTQ is so common it's weird when somebody raises a pierced eyebrow. But other markets are more… traditional. In places like that, don't just go by your experience. You may know the places where you encounter people similar to you, but those are probably not the only places in town. Just because you identify as LGBT or Q, that doesn't mean you only do stuff where people like you go.

There's this neat service called Google that lets you find out all sorts of stuff. Check it out. You might be able to get a good idea of just how many of the other people at the PTA meeting or the sporting goods store identify the way you do.

I'm not saying you should turn this into a science, although I bet someone with a graduate degree and some time could write a pretty popular book by doing so. What I'm saying is that when you know the kind of market you're in, you can set reasonable expectations for the experience you're likely to have.

That's a real thing. Turns out, houses within a quarter-mile of a Starbucks increased in value significantly faster than homes that didn't have a Starbucks nearby, at least according to a study by Zillow.

If the study really did identify a causal relationship (which I'm not qualified to evaluate, even though I know how to throw around terms like "causal relationship"), then finding out that a Starbucks is going to be built in a neighborhood would probably be a good idea if you're buying or selling a house there.

By the way, you don't have to read the *Harvard Business Review* to figure out the general trends of your neighborhood. Look around. See what's happening. Most of the things that affect home prices are common sense. People want to live where it's safe. Where their kids can go to good schools. Where they can shop for clothes and groceries and where they can go out to a movie once in a while. If those things are changing, are they changing for the better or the worse?

As to the region, it mostly comes down to basic economics. In places where there are more people who want homes than there are homes for them to buy, prices go up.

But keep in mind, basic doesn't necessarily mean simple.

A couple of years ago, houses in Portland were in so much demand that they would regularly get multiple offers — all of them over the listing price — within two days of being listed.

The market here has changed, and these days, I don't expect a well-priced listing to get an offer in the first three weeks.

Here's the important part: houses in Portland — all over Portland — are more expensive now. The average sales price of a house here is a crap ton higher than it was three years ago, but it takes longer to get fewer buyers to submit offers.

That may seem like a contradiction, but it isn't. Demand is closer to supply, but the other underlying factors that determine a home's value have made the prices go up.

And no, it isn't because they put a Starbucks in every neighborhood.

Spouse Hunting: Using The Rules Of Real Estate To Find The Love Of Your Life

Rule #12
The Closer a Home Is to Move-In Ready, the More It's Worth

There are exceptions, but most people are looking for a home to move into. The closer it is to being a place they want to live, the more they're willing to pay for it.

An extreme example is land. If you sell an empty lot, you'd be stupid to expect to get as much for it as an equivalent lot that has a house on it. It's not move-in ready.

A construction site is generally worth more because (presumably) a lot of the prep work has been done. Permits have been pulled, plans have been drawn up, surveys have been completed…

A finished house is worth more than a construction site.

Now comes the part that a lot of people don't understand. A house that is lived in is not the same thing as a house that's live-in ready. Nobody wants to move into a place that's full of your crap.

⇩

People have crap the same way houses do. It's called baggage and only delusional people think their potential partner doesn't have stuff they need to deal with, things that are in the way of having an idyllic life.

I'm not saying you should pretend that that's not the case. What I am saying is that you're going to be more attractive if you keep a prospective partner's eye on you, not the crap.

The best way to do that is, of course, to work on yourself. Resolve some of those unresolved issues. You'll never get them all taken care of, but at least you'll be making progress and trust me, progress is sexy.

The other part, though, is really about awareness.

I read a comment on a dating site by a woman who said that her most disastrous first date involved a guy who needed her to drive him to the airport before they went out to dinner so he could pick up a snake.

I don't mean any offense by that. Nobody wants to move into a place that's full of my crap, either, and my crap is special. It's special to me. Just like your crap is special to you.

People want to live with crap that's special to them.

When you're selling your house, you can't know what crap is going to be special to the person who buys it, so rather than try to take out your crap and put in theirs, I recommend that you just take out yours.

Also, I've said this before, but fix the stuff that needs to be fixed.

You may have worked out a really cool way to turn on the bathroom light with a pair of pliers, but someone looking to buy your house is not likely to consider that an advantage. Fix it. Standardize it. I'll get into colors and stuff later and when I do you'll see that I'm not saying to turn your house into one just like every other house out there. But if stuff could stand to be working better, make sure that it is.

That's clutter.

Sure, somebody might think that that's move-in ready, but chances are? Not even close.

That's move-in ready.

If the person who buys your house really wants to use a pair of pliers to turn on the bathroom light, let them unfix it.

Rule #13
Figure Out Who You're Marketing To

You're not marketing your home to everyone. In fact, you're not marketing your home to everyone looking for a home. So don't waste your time and money getting your message out to the wrong people.

The first question to ask yourself is, "Who are the right people?"

If you're selling a four-bedroom house in the suburbs, it's probably families. If you're selling an industrial loft downtown, it could be young professionals.

The second question to ask yourself is "Who are the people who are connected to the right people?" Everybody knows somebody and I bet if you gave it some thought you could think of people who know people who might want to buy your house.

⇩

This isn't about creating your messaging (that's Rule #17 through #27, mostly). It's about who you're going to get it out to. You have two audiences. The first — most important — audience is the people you hope to attract (Rule #5). The second audience is people who can get your message out to your first audience.

Who are they?

You know that thing about six degrees of separation? The idea is that everybody knows somebody who is connected to people who are connected to people in such a way that you are six connections or fewer from anybody. That means you already know people who can connect you with The One.

Figure out who they are.

Once you've done that, all you have to do is get your message out to them in a way that they get your message out to their connections. How hard could that be?

⇩

My client who was confined to a wheelchair? Her home was handicap accessible. She had a ramp to the front door and a roll-in shower. So of course I got the word out to organizations and people who work with disabled people.

Well, pretty hard, actually. But hard isn't the same as impossible. Which brings us to….

Rule #14
Get Help

I meet a lot of people who want to sell their homes themselves. They think that paying a commission to someone like me is throwing money away.

Since this is my book, I'm going to tell you why it isn't.

First, I do this for a living. How many houses have you sold? Are you up to date on current real estate law? Do you know what forms need to be filled out, where they need to be filed, who they need to be filed with, and when?

Second, are you tuned in to the market? Not just in the short term, meaning you've seen that Zillow projects prices in your neighborhood to rise by 1.8% over the next year. Have you identified the trends in neighborhoods? Can you spot the patterns of gentrification?

We all want love to just happen. And sometimes it does. I met my ex-wife in an airport. The woman I was with before her? I met her at an electronics store.

I don't go to bars and I don't go to church, so with those two notable exceptions, almost all of the women I ended up going out with were people I met at work.

The thing is, none of those relationships worked out.

Oh, some weren't terrible. I'm still very close friends with the woman I met at work. But we're no longer together, so even though it worked out, it didn't, you know, work out.

As for the others, we're either vaguely in touch or communicating far too often through the Multnomah County Court System. So it seems to me that maybe I shouldn't be doing this alone. Maybe, like with real estate, I could benefit from having an expert guide me.

The first step is Internet dating sites. They're like the Multiple

Third, how are your negotiating skills? No matter how good they are, I can tell you from my own experience that it's easier to be an effective negotiator for someone else than it is for yourself.

Fourth, how many of the tricks of the business do you really understand? Two offers may be for the same amount, but one can end up costing you tens of thousands of dollars when you get into the weeds in it.

Fifth, when you get into the weeds, who's going to help you out? It's not going to be me. Not unless you pay me not just my regular commission, but a bonus to try and undo the mess you've gotten yourself into.

Sixth, are you aware of the ways to protect yourself during the process? No, I'm not going to tell you what those are.

Seventh, who are your resources? Got a title company you trust? An inspector you can rely on? Who do you call for your sewer scopes? Your radon tests? I have my list. It's a list I've built over the

⬇

Listing Service of relationships when you think about it. And if you buy that analogy, putting up a profile is similar to listing your property yourself.

It's a pretty good parallel and it holds up until the point where you ask, "So what's the equivalent of the real estate agent in this transaction?"

I don't know.

course of my career and I've got it to the point where I know that the person I bring in is going to do an excellent job for an excellent price.

If you're buying a house, it's even stupider to try to do it alone. Our system is set up so that the seller of a property pays a commission to the listing agent and it's the listing agent who compensates the buyer's agent.

I don't agree with that system, but that's the way it is. And what it means is that if you're buying a house, you're not likely to save any money by going solo.

That's because the listing agent is going to pocket the entire commission. You can try to negotiate that down, but you're actually at a legal disadvantage if you try. The listing agent has a contract with the seller that was in place long before you come along with your offer. That contract spells out how much of a commission they make. When you try to get the listing agent to change the commission they're paid by the seller, you're asking them to renegotiate a contract

⇩

they have with someone else. On the speculative chance that your transaction is going to close.

Not likely.

That's a lot of negative, so let me give you some positive.

A good realtor can read between the lines of a listing and often will be able to figure out just how desperate a seller is. A good realtor can turn you on to ways to maximize your return. A good realtor is only paid when a transaction closes, so they have an incentive to make sure the deal closes. A good realtor has experience with sales and will help you position your home in the market. A good realtor has tons of resources — buyers, investors, other realtors — and can get your property in front of people you can't. Or can put the word out to people you don't know about the place you're looking to buy. A good realtor has tons of other resources — contractors, gardeners, painters, cleaners, stagers, lenders, escrow officers, etc. People they've worked with before. People they know to be reliable, trustworthy, and

⇩

inexpensive. A good realtor knows the market. And knows what's standard operating procedure. A good realtor will manage the process. A good realtor knows other realtors — their reputations and their approaches — as well as other brokerages. They know which ones work with shady suppliers and which ones like to list their properties at the high end.

The reason people like me do this job is because it is a job. You already have a job. Do you really want to learn how to do a second job for the sole purpose of completing one transaction? Don't get me wrong, I don't want you to be ignorant. I love working with knowledgeable clients. I just don't require it.

I know. You can't help but wonder if I'm earning all that money that I'm getting paid for helping you sell or buy a house. You believe I know multiple ways to rip you off.

I do.

But I'm not going to. I don't do that. I don't do that not just

because it's wrong, but because I'm greedy. I want you to come back to me when you're ready to buy or sell your next house. And the one after that. I'm going to make more money off of you by working with you multiple times — and by doing such a good job that you refer me to all your friends — than I could possibly make by ripping you off on this one transaction.

And you know what else? I'm actually going to work my ass off to keep you from getting ripped off by all the other players in the process who also know how to rip you off. Convincing a new client to work with me is hard. It's a lot easier to convince someone who's worked with me before, who's seen how hard I try, to trust me again.

Oh, and no, I'm not willing to cut my commission. You want a discount, go to a discount brokerage.

Rule #15
You Can't Step into the Same River Twice

According to a study by Redfin, Portland has about 500,000 single family homes.

And right now, 1,630 of those are for sale.

A year ago, there were 2,682 homes for sale. I can't give you an exact figure, but I guarantee you that the vast majority of those were not the same homes that were for sale a year later.

Just about 2,682 people found homes to buy. Their dream homes. The ones they'd been looking for.

If they'd been looking a year later, like now, they'd still find homes to buy. Their dream homes. The ones they'd been looking for.

See what I'm getting at here?

In 2017, the population of Portland was 647,805. There's no direct way to tell how many of those people were in relationships, but according to (https://www.bestplaces.net/compare-cities/portland_or/san_diego_ca/people), 56.9% of the population is single.

Even if 1/2 of those don't identify as the gender you're attracted to and 1/2 of the ones remaining are not attracted to people of your particular gender identity and 90% of the remaining people are either too young or too old for you, your odds of finding love are more than five times better than they are of finding a house.

That's kind of reassuring, isn't it?

And you know what? A year from now, the numbers will probably be pretty much the same. But the people won't be. A lot of folks will get married or move in together. And a lot of people will get divorced, split up, or kill each other.

Same river, only totally different.

Rule #16
Always Be Ready to Show

You never know when the right buyer is going to come along, so you need to be prepared. Constantly prepared.

Get rid of those pizza boxes on the coffee table. Run the vacuum cleaner, then put it away. Pay those bills stacked up on the dining room table. Take out the trash. Do something about that smell.

If you're selling your home, anybody who stops by could be a buyer. If they're not, they might know somebody who's looking.

Brush your goddamn hair. Brush your goddamn teeth. Don't wear those ratty jeans. Take a shower. Even if you're just going to the grocery store. Hell, even if you're staying at home.

Be prepared for the next person to turn the corner to be The One.

Yeah, I know it's a long shot. But hey, what if it actually does happen? Do you really want to take that risk?

Rule #17
Think Benefits, Not Features

Back in Rule #7, I had you create a list of characteristics that your house — the one you're selling — possesses. The next step is to think of the feelings created by those things.

A house that's set back from the road feels private.

One that's near an on-ramp is an easy commute.

A house that hasn't been maintained is an opportunity to make it your own.

A small house is easy to maintain, while a big house gives you room to expand.

See what I'm doing there?

There's an adage in advertising: Sell the sizzle, not the steak. What sizzle does your property have?

As you go through your list of characteristics — Rule #7, that list of things that define you — you're going to find some positive ones. Those are easy to convert from features into benefits.

If you're honest with yourself, you'll also come up with a bunch of things that you think make you less desirable. And if you're like most people, you're going to be tempted to spiral into self-doubt.

Stop.

You don't have negative characteristics.

You have characteristics.

You're old? Someone out there is looking for a partner with life experience.

You have cancer? Someone out there is looking for a partner who understands their own struggle.

I'm serious. Lots of people out there are looking for what you offer. You just have to be sure to understand that you do have lots to offer.

Rule #18
Staging Makes a Difference

🏠

Back when I used to direct films and commercials, I had basically two choices: I could shoot scenes on location or I could have my team create a set and dress it to look the way I wanted it to.

I learned a super important lesson. Real life rarely looks as good as something stylized.

And because it doesn't look as good, it isn't worth as much.

Real life is messy. You have to hang your coat somewhere when you come in the door and you probably toss your bills onto a pile on the kitchen counter so you can remember that they need to be paid. You don't bother decanting your olive oil into a pretty crockery thing and even if you do, it probably doesn't match the container you have your Mediterranean sea salt in.

When you're listing your home, you have three choices, not two like we do in film.

⇩

When it comes to finding a partner, you are the equivalent of the house. So how are you presenting yourself?

• You could go out into the world just the way you are, but seriously, look in the mirror and tell me if how you look right now makes the impression you want to make.

That's as is, and it's going to get you the fewest offers.

• You could go around naked. The upside is that you'll be making an honest presentation of yourself. The downside is that the dating pool in jail isn't all that deep. Skip this one.

• You can find the clothes that best represent the best possible you.

I'm not saying that you should wear suits or party dresses. But if you're selling yourself as outdoorsy, dress outdoorsy. If you're selling yourself as thoughtful, dress thoughtfully.

No, I don't know what that means.

• You can show it the way it is, the way you live in it. The way it is will generate the lowest offers. People want a fantasy, not a reality, and sorry, seeing your home the way it is doesn't lend itself to a fulfilling fantasy.

• You can empty it out and show it as a blank canvas. Empty will generate better offers because at least people don't have to get past what's in there. But they do have to use their imaginations to picture what it could be like.

• You can empty it out and then build it back as a stylized version of a place somebody will dream of living. In real estate, we call that Staged — meaning somebody with an eye comes in and puts together a cohesive, aspirational environment based on the feelings you came up with in the last rule. Staged is where you get the best offers.

Staged is actually a really good name for what it is because it's essentially what we do when we create a set on a stage for filming. We

⇩

create an idealized version of reality, where all the constituent

elements contribute to a cohesive message.

Rule #19
Price Well

When you list a house, you set a price. An exact number that you're telling the market that you think it's worth. But the reality is a little more complicated.

I can run the numbers a dozen different ways, but I'm not going to tell you that your home is worth some exact price. What I'm going to give you is a range.

The reason is that even if I can take into consideration all the factors at play when I price the house — comparative homes that have sold, perceptions of the neighborhood, perceptions of your lot, interest rates, trends in population, and other stuff — factors can change overnight. I've listed a house only to see another, similar house down the street get listed for $15,000 less just ten minutes later.

The difference in pricing made sense. My sellers weren't in a huge hurry, but the people who owned the other house had to move

⬇

How much of a hurry are you in? What do you expect the trends will be? Is there a lot of market action right now? Ask yourself these questions as you figure out just what your "price" is. And when I say "price," I mean what you want versus what you are willing to accept to form a long-term relationship with somebody.

When I lived in Hollywood, where attractive women are a dime a dozen and men who work as directors are "worth" more because there are so few, it was easy for me to date hot women. And yeah, at the time it was an important criterion for me. I used to joke about having casting sessions for my next date.

Pretty disgusting, I know. I got my comeuppance, thanks to the hottie I fell for who screwed me out of my kids and my savings, so you don't have to feel like I deserve to be loathed.

Anyway.

If your "price" is high, don't expect offers to come in very quickly. If your "price" is low, they still might not come in quickly. It

out of town. But as far as buyers were concerned it was two equivalent homes asking significantly different amounts.

As it turned out, the other house's low price brought tons of buyers into the neighborhood. The house sold pretty quickly, but all of those other buyers except one didn't get it. Thanks at least in part to the additional traffic that other house generated, we ultimately ended up accepting an offer above listing.

When you see my range, you have a couple of choices. You can price the house toward the bottom of the range and if you do that, you can expect a pretty good number of showings and maybe multiple offers. You can price toward the top of the range and if you do that, you can expect fewer showings and not so many offers. Or you can disregard what I recommend and come up with your own listing price.

If the market thinks your price is high, you can always come down.

If the market thinks your price is low, you'll be able to work the price up.

depends on a lot of factors.

And like I tell my clients, all you need is one good buyer to make a sale.

Hey, you know what? I'm going to make that its own rule.

If the market thinks your price is way off the mark, the market will think there's something seriously wrong with either you (if the price is too high) or the house (if the price is too low).

Rule #20
You Only Need One Buyer/Seller

You're not looking to collect pieces like on a Monopoly board. You're looking for a home. One home.

All you need is one.

So if there's one home for sale and it's perfect for you, all you have to do is make sure nobody else gets it.

If there are thousands of homes for sale and dozens of them are right for you, all you have to do is look at them all, figure out which one suits you best, make the most appropriate offer, and negotiate well. If it all works out, great. If not, move on to number two.

If you're selling a home and there's only one buyer out there, but that buyer is perfect for your home, all you have to do is make sure they don't want any other home more.

If there are thousands of buyers out there and dozens of them are looking for the one you're selling, all you have to do is establish a

⬇

Which would you rather do? Go out on one date a night for 365 nights and meet the right person in a year? Or go out on one date a year from now and meet the right person then?

If you're like most people, you said you'd rather go on one date. But if you're like most people, what you choose to do is go on as many dates as you can.

The truth is, it doesn't matter which approach you take if they're both going to get you to the same outcome. But going on dates feels like progress, so that's what we choose.

It's not progress.

I mean, yeah. It can be fun. And there are things that are more fun with someone else. Even if it isn't the right someone else. But ultimately, the thing you're trying to accomplish here is to find The One.

Keep your eye on the ball. The prize. The ball prize. You know

⇩

price that makes your home more appealing than any other. That doesn't necessarily mean lower, by the way. The more unique your home is, the more the right buyers will be willing to pay. The most appealing price is the one that generates the most interest among the most suitable buyers.

If you get multiple offers, you can often use one against the other in order to work the price up. And once you accept an offer, you can ask other buyers to be in backup position, which means if the first transaction doesn't close, they have dibs.

Bottom line, though, is that one house will be sold to one buyer (or, you know, family). You only need one of either to have success.

what I mean. You decided back in Rule #3 that you wanted a relationship.

A relationship. A. One.

Rule #21
The One Factor That Has <u>Nothing</u> to Do with What Your Home Will Sell for Is What You Think It's Worth

Myriad factors go into determining what a house is worth: supply, demand, population trends, gentrification trends, zoning laws, lot size, interest rates, construction costs, number of bedrooms, labor costs, employment, availability of credit, number of bathrooms, alternative uses of money, foreign investment, view, design trends, lifestyle trends, commuting factors, paint colors, noise levels, neighbors who park old appliances on their front yards… All those things and more combine to determine what a buyer is likely to offer.

The one thing that has absolutely nothing to do with the price you get is what you think it's worth.

Nobody cares that you put $80,000 into the living room. Or that you paid $645,000 for the house. Nobody gives a crap that you have

You know what you want. You want somebody intelligent, but not too much smarter than you. Ambitious, but not so driven that you don't get to spend time together. Gorgeous, but who also thinks you're stunning. You want clear skin, kind eyes, a delightful laugh, and an ability to make you laugh.

That's what we all want.

Unfortunately, you might not be able to get that.

Are you willing to stay single if you don't? Because this is the harsh truth: the "price" you think you deserve might not be the price you can get.

to pay off your son's student loans or that you don't have any money saved up for retirement.

Sorry.

That's not to say you don't get to have a price in mind. You can put any price you want on it.

But if nobody is willing to pony up, you better be willing to keep it.

Rule #22
Don't Skimp on Photography

With a smartphone, pretty much anybody can snap a shot that's exposed correctly and in focus. But there's a lot more to photography than that. Good photographers — and I know this stuff because I used to work as a pro photographer — also take photos that are composed well. They control light and shadow. They use focal length, camera height, and camera angle to present space. They avoid distracting crap in the frame. And most important, they capture what I like to think of as a critical moment.

Back in Rule #17, I talked about turning features into benefits. If you don't believe photography plays a role here, you're missing a huge opportunity.

You know how your house feels to you. Thanks to Rule #17, you know how you want it to feel to others.

It's possible you're going to convey that feeling by snapping a

What is it with bathroom selfies? I see those on almost every single dating profile I look at and you know what they tell me?

They tell me that you have no friends. And that you think a bathroom is the best environment to communicate that you love the outdoors or enjoy quiet nights by the fire.

I'm not going to insist that you hire a pro because 1) it feels kinda creepy and 2) a lot pros don't know how to make photos that don't look polished to the point that you'll come across as a product. So if you decide to hire a pro, hire one who's good at profile photos.

But if you decide not to hire a pro, find a friend. If you don't have a friend, put down this book, get out into the world, and don't come back until you have at least two people in your life to whom you can admit that you're looking for a life partner to and who you know will help you find that person.

Go out with your friends. Or stay in with them. Whatever. They're your friends. You like doing stuff with them.

shot. But it's more likely that you're not.

Hire a pro. Just do it.

In addition to all the other reasons, which I listed above, a pro will remove stuff that detracts from the message. A pro will know what time of day will present your home best. And a pro will have the technical knowledge to create versions of photos that will best present themselves in whatever medium you're using them in.

Ask them to occasionally take photos of you doing the things you like to do. If you really like to do those things, you might actually be smiling.

Smiling is attractive.

Some other tips:

Guys, I know you like to fish. Keep it to one shot of you holding a fish.

Women, I know you love to do yoga. Keep it to one yoga pose.

What I'm trying to say is that your personality is more important than your activity. Show your personality. You can show it doing an activity. But don't let the activity be a substitute for a personality.

Rule #23
Put Thought Into Preparing Your Listing

A listing is an official statement. It's you proclaiming to the world that you are actively pursuing a sale.

If that makes you uncomfortable, you're not ready.

Assuming you're ready, wouldn't you want your listing to make that statement both loud and clear?

You have photos. You know what features the home has. You know what benefits your features promise. All you have to do now is write it up.

Well, not you. Your agent. Me. Or whoever.

Make sure the copy sounds like it's actually true to your house. More fundamentally, that it's actually true.

And this is important. Have someone proofread it. Like my mom, for example. She used to teach grammar and composition and

Just like a listing is an official statement proclaiming to the world that you are actively pursuing the sale of a house, a dating profile is a proclamation that you're looking for a partner.

Or should be.

You have photos. You know what attributes you have. You know what benefits those attributes promise. All you have to do now is write it up.

If you can, write it yourself. Your own voice is a better representation of who you are than a bathroom selfie. If you can't, find someone who will write it with your voice in mind.

But even more important than with a real estate listing, have someone proofread it. Not my mom, though.

This is when you should definitely stop by the local college and offer a grad student ten bucks to proofread the listing. You're always ready to show, right? You might meet someone…

If that makes you uncomfortable, you're not ready.

she catches all sorts of stuff.

If my mom's not available, call your old English teacher. Hell, stop by the local college and offer a grad student ten bucks to proofread the listing. You might not know the difference between "it's" and "its" or "they're," "their," and "there," and most of the people reading the listing might not know or care, either, but the ones that do? Their likely to judge you. And there money is good.

Rule #24
Avoid Clichés Like the Plague

See what I did there?

Come on, that's funny!

Whatever.

I did it to make a point and the point is that while clichés serve a useful purpose — they condense a complicated thought into a simple expression — they inadvertently demonstrate a lack of imagination. They make you come across as lazy.

With all the homes that are sold, it's hard to come up with a new way to describe four bedrooms and two bathrooms, but hey, isn't that what we're getting paid to do?

I don't care how hot you are; if I see the words "Living life to the fullest" in your online profile, I'm swiping left.

Now to be fair, lack of imagination is a Deal Breaker for me. It might not be for you. Maybe you're looking for someone who speaks in clichés.

Or maybe you never thought about it this way:

You're competing with every other profile out there for the attention of the person you want to meet. So if you and some other person both use clichés like "as comfortable in high heels as you are in hiking boots," what makes you more appealing than the other man? Or woman? Either.

Rule #25
Everything Means Nothing

You can't be small and large, serious and funny, active and lazy. They're contradictions.

I mean, yes, we're all contradictions. But we're more one thing than another.

The thing that's more? That's what gets people interested. The thing that's less, but that's still there? That's what satisfies people's needs for completeness.

I see listings all the time that promise "The best of urban and country living." Um, no. The best thing about urban living is that it exactly isn't country living.

You're not going to attract more potential buyers by trying to find things to appeal to everybody. You're only going to dilute the things that make you appealing to the most likely buyers.

⬇

"I love going out and staying in."

"I enjoy everything from dive bars to fine dining."

"I listen to every kind of music."

Who are these people? I'm serious. I can't tell a damn thing about you if you don't narrow it down.

It's okay not to love everything, be up for anything. In fact, you don't even have to mention what you aren't/don't like/don't do/can't do. But there's gotta be stuff that you're more of than other things. Things you like more. Things you'd rather do.

What I'm saying is that it's okay to like hiking. Liking hiking doesn't mean you hate wearing high heels. It means you actually like something.

You ever listen to Tony Robbins? He makes a really valid point in his thing about Six Human Needs (https://www.tonyrobbins.com/mind-meaning/why-you-are-the-way-you-are/). He says we're all

⇩

If your house is large, let it be large. Not large but also small.
Somebody who wants a small house isn't going to want your large
house. And somebody who wants a large house is going to conclude
that your house isn't really large.

driven by a desire for certainty, variety, significance, love and connection, growth/contribution, and what makes you do what you do.

Here's where it gets cool. Some of those human needs are in direct conflict with each other. Like certainty and variety. The more certainty you need, the less variety you can have.

He's not saying that you can't value both and neither am I. The important part is to know what you value most and lead with that.

Leave the nuance for when you're getting to know each other.

Rule #26
Show, Don't Say

There ought to be a saying. Something about how a picture is worth, oh, I don't know, 934 words or something.

Seeing something saves you a lot of trouble having to explain it.

I saw a listing once that said the house had "walls of glass." There were no pictures of walls of glass. (The reason, I found out when I saw the place, was that there actually were no walls of glass.) If there had been a picture, I wouldn't have needed the words.

You see listings all the time that describe a house as "beautiful" or "charming."

Like using those words is going to make me believe that, yes, that house really is beautiful or charming.

Come on. People aren't that stupid. Only marketing directors are that stupid. Marketing directors actually believe it's okay to tell

Pop quiz time. You want to convince potential partners that you're fit. In your dating profile, should you A) Mention that you're fit, or B) Post a picture that shows how fit you are?

And yet. 90% of the profiles I see do A. And then go on to show a gallery full of bathroom selfies — usually ones where they're scowling at the camera as the shutter goes off.

Ugh.

But what if that thing is intangible? Same thing goes, only swap out the word "demonstrate" for "show" if that helps make it clearer. I can't tell you how many dating profiles I see where the person says, "I'm witty."

Really? You can't think of a wittier way to make that point?

And for god's sake, don't tell me what I can already see. I come across profiles all the time where the women tell me they're attractive, blonde, thin…

⇩

people that their product is "New And Improved." Think about it. If something is new, it can't be improved. And if it's improved, how the fuck can it be new?

Don't be a marketing director. You're better than that.

I know what you're thinking. You're thinking, "Okay, smartass. So how come your book is all words and no pictures?"

Because the second, implicit part is "if you can."

Show if you can. If you can't, then you say.

Here's the thing. It's either true or it's not. If it's true, you don't have to tell me. If it's not, you're either a liar or self-unaware. Both of which, I'm sorry, are Deal Breakers.

Rule #27

You're Not Selling a House, You're Selling a Lifestyle

That thing I said about sizzle and steak — remember that? — this is how you ratchet it up to the next level.

Take those features that you've turned into benefits and ask yourself, how do they fit together?

The answer is lifestyle.

That's what you're selling.

The house isn't the end. It's the means. What you're saying to the buyer is "this is the life you'll get to live if you buy this house." Pull that off and you can price high, negotiate hard, and do really well.

I know. I've done this. I sold a fixer-upper as an opportunity to step back in time. I sold a dinky little house as a way to while away your days wandering through the neighborhood. I sold a well-maintained little old lady's home as a way to live without a care.

Think back to the last time you were in love. You didn't fantasize about the person. You fantasized about being with that person.

I'm right, aren't I?

Of course I am. That's why it was so painful when they didn't call. Why you'd agonize over what they were doing when you weren't with them.

What makes one person more exciting than another? It's not who they are, what they look like, what they do. It's the life they offer. Your life, with them.

Once you've done that, turn it around. What life are you offering?

It's not enough to be smart, funny, adventurous, and fit. All that can add up to boring. You need to promise something more.

⇩

All three of those had multiple offers and all of them ultimately sold for more than the listing price.

I can't tell you what that something more is, I can just tell you that when you figure that out, you'll be able to price high, negotiate hard, and do really well.

Rule #28

Your Listing Is Not Meant to Sell the House

I know. You're selling something extremely valuable. People should take the time to read your listing carefully so they can make an informed decision.

But it doesn't work that way.

There's a misconception that real estate agents are in the business of selling houses. We're not. We're in the business of selling showings.*

Your listing is there to serve one purpose: to encourage a buyer to find out more. I write listings with the sole intention of grabbing a buyer's attention and compelling them to see the house.

The listing doesn't sell the house, it sells the showing. It's the showing that sells the house.

---

* We're also in the business of analyzing market conditions, advising clients on strategy, providing reliable resources, managing the sales process, keeping paperwork in order, adhering to timelines and legal requirements, negotiating transactions, making sure all the different players involved in a transaction have the information they need when they need it, and holding people's hands during what can be an extraordinarily stressful process.

You would think that someone looking for the person to spend the rest of their life with would give a dating profile more than a cursory glance, but nope. This isn't where thoughtful decisions are made. When people look at a dating profile, they aren't making a choice between Yes and No.

They're making a choice between No and Maybe.

There's no coming back from No. So do what you can to get to Maybe.

Maybe will give your potential partner a chance to look deeper. That's what the first date is.

Be intriguing. Be real. Present your best self. And don't get into negative shit.

Encourage potential partners to want to find out more.

But — and this is important — don't ever misrepresent. You want them to find out more. And when they do, you don't want them to feel deceived.

Spouse Hunting: Using The Rules Of Real Estate To Find The Love Of Your Life

Remember what I said about showing versus saying? If you deceive someone into going out on a date with you, you're showing them that you're deceitful.

Rule #29
Get the Word Out

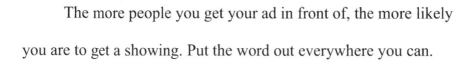

The more people you get your ad in front of, the more likely you are to get a showing. Put the word out everywhere you can.

One of the benefits of working with a realtor is the way we can get your listing out. Not just on the MLS, and not just onto Zillow and Redfin. We have networks — the better ones of us, anyway — networks of buyers, investors, other realtors. We have access to circles you don't have access to.

We put signs in the yard and we hold open houses.

I happen to have a background in marketing, so in addition to those other things, I do advertising and put the word out using social media.

I'm not saying to be indiscriminate. It's also important to put the message where it'll reach the most likely prospects. But make sure you reach those prospects.

⇩

You already know about Match.com, eHarmony, Tinder, OK Cupid, JDate, Christian Mingle, Ship...

Get on all of them. Or all of them that you feel comfortable on.

But also make sure your friends and family know not just that you're looking, but what you're looking for. Mention it to your coworkers.

I'm not saying that you should get a T-shirt that says, "I'm single — want to go on a date?" What I am saying is that people can only react to the information they have. The fact that you're looking for a partner is information.

For god's sake, don't let it dominate every conversation. Think about it this way: When someone asks what your interests are, they should come away with a good idea of the things you like to do. But it wouldn't hurt to let them know you'd love to have a partner to do them with.

Remember, those buyers want to buy the house you're selling.

But that's not going to happen if they don't know it's for sale.

Rule #30
Have Someone Else Hold the Showing

You don't want to be there when strangers go poking around in your house. They might hate it. And even if they love it, they might pretend to hate it as a ploy to get you to lower your price.

Give your agent the keys, take your kids to the movies, and relax.

Most showings come to nothing. That's hard to stomach when you're the homeowner hoping hoping hoping that this buyer will be the one. (Don't skip ahead, but Rule #37 is about stinking of desperation.)

When it comes to finding a partner, it's impossible to have someone else show you without you being there. Sorry.

You pretty much have to go on dates.

But you can still do it in such a way that a presumably objective other person can point up your highlights and address criticisms. I like to call this the Double Date and brilliant though the idea sounds, no, I didn't come up with it.

Remember those friends you have? Especially on your first date, make arrangements for them to be with you. Them being a couple. It's awkward bringing your single same-gender friend along on a date. Even awkwarder bringing an opposite-gender friend along. Akwardest of all would be bringing a group of single same-gender friends along.

If all of your friends are single, maybe you're in a group. I know, it feels weird to invite a date to join a group, especially a group where everybody is pretty tight, but think about it. If the group likes

you, they'll do what a broker does at a showing. And if they're tight, then maybe you don't make it an official get-together. Maybe you ask a couple of them to work as your "broker" (although maybe you shouldn't use that word).

If the date goes well, then people you trust are already there to help you evaluate. And if it goes badly, hey, at least you got to get together with people you like.

Rule #31
A Seller Controls Three Things: Price, Condition, and Access

There's only so much you can do when you're selling your property. You can change the price. You can fix the place up. And you can make your place available for buyers to look at.

There's a price at which any property will get an offer. That price may be lower than you want to get, in which case you simply don't sell. But you can make that price higher by making sure the property is in good condition. And even higher if buyers actually get a chance to see it.

So if you want to maximize the price, improve the property and for god's sake, don't make it hard for people to get in to see it.

I'm going to say it again. When it comes to matters of the heart, "price" does not mean money*. It means value.

You demand a certain value — stuff you require in order to enter into a relationship. For me, those things include integrity, creativity, fun, optimism, and an appreciation of things that are quirky. If I also want clear skin and a willingness to travel, I'm going to have to improve my condition (so I exercise pretty much every day and run a couple times a week, I see my doctor regularly, I don't smoke, and I try to get a decent night's sleep).

I'll be honest, though. Where I'm having a hard time is access. I'm an introvert. Not only that, but I'm an introvert in a business that requires me to work with people. So I simply don't have the energy to go out as much as I should.

I'm not providing as much access as I should.

* Unless you're dating my ex-wife. Don't date my ex-wife

No buyer is going to buy a house without first getting a chance to see it, and no partner is going to settle down with me without first going on a date or two. I know this. Now you do, too.

Rule #32
Don't Be Stupid, Be Safe

Real estate agents have tools to keep them safe when they're showing houses. Some of us learn karate. Some carry pepper spray. Some use smartphone apps that are set up to automatically send an alert to emergency contacts if we don't check in. Others simply let responsible people know where we are, who we're with, and when we expect to be done.

If you're not working with an agent, you're taking on all sorts of risk, the most direct being that you'll probably be in your house, by yourself, when somebody comes to see it.

Most people who come to see a house are legitimately looking for a home. But there are plenty of creeps out there…

This probably goes without saying, but you know me. I'm going to say it anyway: Even though there are a lot of parallels between selling a home and looking for a partner, don't EVER invite a first date over to your home. EVER.

Even if it's me. I mean it.

Meet someplace public. And if you simply can't arrange to make it a group thing or bring friends along, make sure someone you trust knows where you are, who you're with, and when you'll be back. Have them check on you, too, 45 minutes in. Or excuse yourself to use the restroom and make a call.

I like the having-someone-check-on-you thing better. This allows you to prepare a script. One that allows the person calling you to pretend that Aunt Mary just had an aneurism and you need to be back home right away if your date is creeping you out or you're having a hard time making conversation.

Rule #33
Put a Sign Out Front

I've actually had clients tell me they don't want a sign in front. They've explained their reasoning, but none of the explanations make sense. Best I can tell, it comes down to not wanting the neighbors to know that they're selling the house.

Huh?

Like the neighbors aren't going to figure it out when the moving truck pulls up.

If your neighbors like you, don't you think they'd love to help you find a buyer — even if it makes them sad that you're moving? And if your neighbors hate you, don't you think they'd look forward to the opportunity to replace you with somebody better?

A sign in the yard tells more than the neighbors. It tells people driving by. What's the logic behind keeping it secret from them?

I don't get it.

The equivalent of a sign in the yard is not a T-shirt that says, "I'm Single And Looking." As much as we're open to the idea as a society of people searching for love, there's a weird line that you're not supposed to cross. So don't do the T-shirt.

But at the same time, don't wear a wedding ring.

I know, you're hot. You're beating off prospective partners. You get propositioned by homeless people.

I'm calling bullshit on all that.

If you're reading this book, it's because you're looking to find a partner. Which means you haven't had much luck finding one until now. So trust me when I say that putting up a barbed-wire fence doesn't give you the appearance of someone who is open to letting someone in.

The equivalent of putting up a sign is letting people know.

Let people know.

Rule #34

Go Beyond Conventional Channels

I had a client who was confined to a wheelchair. When it came time to list her house, I did all the usual things — listing the property, putting it up in the MLS, advertising on Facebook and Instagram, holding open houses… But I also did other, less conventional things. I contacted all sorts of organizations that worked with handicapped people. I told friends who work in the nonprofit space. I posted on social media, particularly to support groups. I reached out to investors who specialized in building accessible homes or modifying conventional homes for handicapped people.

This is an easy example because an accessible home comes with some obvious attributes that make it interesting to a particular market segment. What would you do with a more conventional home?

Glad you asked.

⬇

Every single day (see what I did there? Single?) you have lots of opportunities to communicate with people who might either be the person you want to meet or know the person you want to meet.

An example.

As a realtor I work with lenders. When someone comes to me wondering if they can qualify for a loan, I pass them along to the lenders I feel are best able to help.

The other day ago I sent another potential client to one of my favorite lenders. I told the lender that I wanted her to take particular care of this potential client, but I always do that. All of my clients deserve particular care and if they don't get it from the lender, I'm not going to refer anybody else.

Anyway. The lender picked up on the comment about giving her special treatment and made a joke about who this client might be. She thought that maybe we were dating.

⇩

If you know me, you know I used to work as a photographer. You also know I keep my chops by going around photographing old cars in Portland. I have more than 2,500 followers on Instagram.

Every time I have a listing, I use my access to that audience. I recently listed a house that had an oversized tandem garage. So I did an Instagram ad campaign emphasizing the garage. Because if you have or like old cars, you might be interested in a house with an oversized garage.

That was direct. But it doesn't always have to be direct.

Earlier in the year, I had a listing without a garage. So I did an Instagram ad campaign to the same audience. The tongue-in-cheek message was that it was an adorable house in an amazing area, but you wouldn't want it. We sold the house for significantly over listing.

I'm not saying that it was definitely the unconventional channels that accounted for the sale. What I'm saying is that unconventional channels can help you get the message out there in interesting ways.

That opened up the conversation. We're not. But I was able to mention to the lender that I was single and that if she happened to know anybody who might be a good fit…

See what I'm saying?

Rule #35
The Most Powerful Advertising Is Word of Mouth

I worked in marketing for years before I got into real estate. Big-time marketing. I rose through the ranks of the most prestigious ad agencies in the world and ultimately held the title of Senior Vice President/Creative Director at BBDO Worldwide, where I was responsible for developing global ad campaigns for Pepsi, Frito-Lay, Visa, Skippy, and Pizza Hut. So I know a thing or two about the power of advertising. And I'm going to let you in on a secret:

Advertising is bullshit.

Advertising can't sell. At best (and the best is rare) it can intrigue. It can motivate someone to find out more. Mostly it can inform — your pizza sauce is chunkier or your hours have been extended. But an ad will never, ever convince.

⇩

Sorry, all you introverts out there (and believe me, I'm about as introverted as they come, so I know) you're not going to find true love without actually meeting potential candidates.

Most of the prospects are going to be wrong for you. That's just the way it is. And if you're not the kind of person who enjoys meeting people who aren't right for you, the entire process can suck.

However.

There are things you can do to narrow the field to more likely prospects and this book is full of them.

Once the field has been narrowed, the best way to improve your chances of a genuine connection is to have somebody else recommend you.

A word from a friend is gold.

Think about it. In every other aspect of your life — finding a babysitter, applying for a job, choosing a laundry detergent — it takes

That's not to say that you don't need to advertise. It's a kind of a baseline, like a brochure or a website. Advertising reassures the market that you're credible.

If you really want to convince or compel, the second-best way to do that is in person. The one and only best way to do that is to have somebody else do that for you. In person.

I've said it before and I'll say it again: The listing doesn't sell the house. It sells the showing.

A listing gets people interested enough to find out more.

What sells the house is the visit. When potential buyers come by and learn about the place in person. When they imagine themselves cooking in the kitchen and waking up in the bedroom.

When they talk to the listing agent or the owners, the neighbors, the other people looking at the house.

This is why we like to get as many people into an open house as we can. If we can get a critical mass of people to show up, they can't

one hell of a resume to overcome the recommendation of somebody

you know. Even if that person has absolutely no authority in the area.

help but talk. When one potential buyer overhears another say, "I like

the tile in the bathroom," I'm 50% more likely to get an offer.

Rule #36
Things to Tell Yourself When Things Look Bleak

"I deserve a home."

"There is a place out there that's right for me."

"If it were too easy, I wouldn't appreciate it when I found it."

"The time I spend looking is time I spend learning."

"Every one that's wrong for me makes it clearer what will be right for me."

"I deserve a partner."

"There is a person out there that's right for me."

"If it were too easy, I wouldn't appreciate them when I found them."

"The time I spend looking is time I spend learning."

"Every one that's wrong for me makes it clearer what will be right for me."

Rule #37
Don't Stink of Desperation

Whenever you see the words "motivated seller," that's an invitation to submit a low-ball offer. That seller is desperate.

The sad thing is, the house is not going to get a lot of offers. And the ones it gets aren't going to be that good.

Desperation is a real turnoff. When the sellers are "motivated," buyers believe there's something wrong with the house.

I sometimes come across dating profiles where the woman will say something like, "Please be employed."

I don't swipe right.

So the poor woman spends another Saturday night alone and wonders why things are so bleak.

They're bleak because you're desperate.

That's not to say they wouldn't be horrible if you weren't, but at least if you weren't, you wouldn't feel so bad about it.

Desperation is tough, though. How do you not feel despair when everyone out there is either a freak or broken? The best way is not to be desperate. And I know, this sounds like it contradicts exactly what I said in Rule #16. But the trick here is to find that fine line — the path where you're single-mindedly determined to accomplish something, but not desperate.

Single-minded determination means, "I'm going to accomplish

Spouse Hunting: Using The Rules Of Real Estate To Find The Love Of Your Life

this." Desperate means, "I'll take anything."

Know the difference. Be the difference.

You might want to start calling me Sensei.

Rule #38
Don't Wait for the Market to Improve

I'm dealing with this right now. I have a client who wants to wait until spring to sell his house. He's convinced the market will be better then.

He may be right.

He may not.

The reality is that he doesn't know. A lot of things can happen between now and spring. Interest rates could go up, which puts downward pressure on home prices. Owners of rental properties could dump their homes because a new rent control law coming into effect in March is so draconian that investors fear that it will severely reduce their ability to turn a profit. A recession could hit. A presidential election could be underway, and the acrimony on both sides could cause tremendous uncertainty.

⇩

As I write this, every single one of those scenarios is not just possible, but likely.

And there are other scenarios that nobody can foresee. An asteroid could hit Portland. Two trucks carrying radioactive waste could collide in the Pearl District. The Willamette River could catch fire. He could be killed by a raging bike commuter wearing a unicorn costume. (As I edit this, I'm sheltering at home thanks to a pandemic that has cratered the economy and threatens millions of lives around the world. Didn't see that coming.)

Of course, other stuff could happen that would have a positive effect. And let's say they do. Let's say the housing market improves so much that his house is suddenly worth 25% more.

So is every other house. So anything he's going to buy is more expensive, too.

The point is that he doesn't know. I don't know, either. All anybody knows for sure is how things are now.

Will you be healthier in the spring? You may be working on it, but you could have a heart attack.

Will you have more money in a year? You might win the lottery, but you might be robbed.

Will the dating pool be bigger in three years? It might, but half the population of people you're interested in could be wiped out by a new disease that hasn't even been identified.*

You don't know.

Things could be better. Things could be worse. Either way, wouldn't you rather have a partner to share that with?

* I wrote the first draft of this book — including these exact words — in October of 2019. And here I am, sheltering in place in my home in April 2020. Friggin' prescient.

Rule #39
Don't Waste Your Time on Unqualified Buyers

When someone wants to take a look at a property I represent, the first thing I need to know is where they are in the process. If they aren't ready, willing, and able to buy a home, we're both wasting our time.

That's not to say I blow them off. I have tons of resources that can help someone who's emotionally ready to become financially ready. But until they're both — emotionally and financially ready — they either can't or won't commit.

As fun as it is to go look at houses, it's also a job.

Remember way back when I told you that the first thing you need to do is get prequalified? That goes for the person you're looking for, too.

Don't date someone who isn't single.

Don't date someone who hasn't figured out who they are and what they want.

Don't date someone who doesn't have the resources to commit (time, money, interest, desire…).

You can't always know these things right off the bat. But you can do your best to find out. And if you do find out that the person you're interested in isn't ready, willing, and able, cut it off and move on. I'm serious. Potential partners are like buses. Another one will come along (you'll see when you get to Rule #52).

Rule #40

Always Consider Highest and Best Use

In real estate, we have a concept of "highest and best use." That means the reasonable, probable, and legal use of a property that is 1) physically possible, 2) appropriately supported, 3) financially feasible, and 4) most profitable.

A couple of interesting points:

Physically possible is important. You can't put a cattle ranch on a suburban lot. Financially feasible is also important. Even if you could put a cattle ranch on a suburban lot, would it make financial sense?

This has nothing to do with what the neighbors want.

What do you want in a partner? I think it's fair to assume we all want the same thing: someone who will help us become the best we can be. Somebody we want the same thing for.

That's highest and best use.

Rule #41
Hold an Open House

One of the best ways to get people to see a property is to invite them.

I know, that sounds stupid basic, but there it is.

Hold an open house. Then hold another one.

Give people an opportunity to get inside and picture what their lives would be like if they lived there.

I like to play music that feels appropriate to the house and serve food that feels consistent, too. Cookies, maybe. Granola. Depends on the house and the neighborhood.

That way, when people come to see the house, they get a multi-sensory idea of what life in the house might be like.

In dating, the analog of an open house is, well, dating.

Go on dates.

Go places you actually want to go — it's silly to meet a date at a sake tasting if you abhor sake. More than silly, actually. It's counterproductive. It's misrepresentation.

A date is an opportunity to give prospective partners a multi-sensory idea of what life with you might be like. And never forget that this is a two-way street. It's also an opportunity to get a multi-sensory idea of what life with that partner might be like.

Every September, the Vaux's Swifts stop off on their migration to spend the night in a chimney on the grounds of an elementary school on the west side of Portland. And thousands of Portlanders sit on blankets and lawn chairs on the lawn outside the school, munching on picnics as they watch thousands of little birds swirl down into the chimney.

It's a quintessentially Portland thing. And something I really love to do.

One September evening, I invited a date to go.

She showed up late, paid no attention to the birds, and wanted to leave early.

It was sad because she was attractive, interesting, intelligent, and funny. But an honest appraisal tells me that she's probably not going to be someone whose company I enjoy at some of the things I like to do.

That doesn't eliminate her from contention. But it does give me some important information I can file away. Just as it gave her important information she can file away.

We may go out again. And if we do, I hope we both keep our eye on how we might fit into each other's lives. If it turns out that the fit isn't there, I hope we're both mature enough to acknowledge the fact and move on.

⇩

Spouse Hunting: Using The Rules Of Real Estate To Find The Love Of Your Life

Oh, and here's a hot tip. If you have a hard time coming up with something more interesting than getting coffee together, it's okay to ask for help. From your date. From your friends. Even from people who actually get paid to come up with date ideas. Just make sure that whatever you end up doing is something you really are interested in doing.

Rule #42
Get Feedback From Buyers

When you're selling a house, you're going to get No a lot more than Yes or even Maybe. But that's okay. You only need one Yes. And until you get it, No comes with information. Or can, if you bother to ask.

This isn't the same thing as overcoming objections, which unfortunately can be the way it comes across if you're not careful. That's why I'm careful. I make sure that when I ask for feedback, it's really understood as feedback. I want to know what didn't work for the buyer. Because maybe it's something that can be addressed.

If it can't, that's fine. A house can't be all things to all people. But if there's a pattern to the responses, you might want to save potential buyers time by alerting them that there's something that might make the house not right for them.

This is hard. You go out with someone and there's no magic. What do you do?

The answer comes down to what do you want?

If you're truly looking for The One, then every person you meet who isn't The One doesn't count as a failure. It counts as an opportunity.

It's one more person you can use to help connect you with someone who might be the one. And it's one more person who can help you clarify both your communication and your goals.

So what you do is you ask for feedback. And you consider it.

Don't go off changing things up based on every comment you get, but remember how you're keeping notes? You evaluate them; they evaluate you. When you come across someone you think has promise, and that person doesn't think there's promise back, it's fair to ask them — and yourself — what's missing. If you see a pattern, maybe it's something you want to address.

Rule #43
If You Don't Get a Showing in Three Weeks, Make a Change

I said three weeks in the heading and that's only because the market in Portland is pretty active. The market you're in may be different and that's why it's important to go back to Rule #11 — the one where you don't even start until you figure out what kind of market you're in.

In Portland right now, if your listing doesn't get any showings in a week and any offers in three weeks, your price is too high.

Yeah, you could hang on and hope, but the market isn't a single thing. It's a collection of thousands of things. Thousands of buyers who are evaluating prospective homes against each other and checking out the ones that seem the most promising. If nobody's checking your listing out, it's obvious that something needs to change.

Rule #11. Read it again.

Determine what a reasonable amount of time is for you to get some interest.

If your profile isn't getting visitors, if your friends aren't setting you up with anybody, if nobody is knocking on your front door, asking if you're single, you're doing something wrong.

Let me rephrase that. You're not doing something right.

So what is it? Price? Marketing? Access?

Sometimes it's really as simple as getting the word out to as broad an audience as possible. But you need to change something. Because if you change nothing, nothing is likely to change.

With a house, there are very few things you can change. You can't change the structure or the location or the neighborhood. You can change the price and the marketing and the condition.

Rule #44
Don't Fall in Love with Your Listing

What happens if the people who respond to your listing aren't the kind of people you want to sell to?

Trick question. It's a violation of all sorts of laws to discriminate on the basis of race, gender, age, marital status, disability, etc.

Sorry. You don't get to sell to the "right kind" of buyer.

That's not to say you have to take the highest offer. You don't have to sell at all. But if you make a decision that doesn't optimize your return, you should probably be prepared to explain it.

Unlike with the sale of a house, in love, you're allowed to discriminate. In fact, that's kind of ultimately what love is. You're discriminating in favor of one person at the expense of all the others.

That one person is a type. We all are. Even those of us who work super hard not to be a type. And if you're honest and you've done more than skim pretty much every single rule up until this one, you know what type you are and you know what type you're looking for.

And yet.

The reality is that the people you attract are all going to be wrong until you meet the one who's right. But wouldn't it be nice to narrow down the ones that do want to meet you to more likely prospects?

If your marketing is attracting atheists and your faith is important — if you enjoy nothing more than sitting on the couch watching *Seinfeld* reruns and you keep attracting athletes — if you're

allergic to dogs and you keep attracting people who volunteer at the Humane Society — you might need to hone your message. No matter how clever it is.

A good message isn't good because you like it. It's good because it communicates the right thing to the right audience.

Rule #45
Disclose Everything You Know

In Oregon, people who sell their homes are required to fill out a seven-page form that tells a prospective buyer about all the material flaws they know about the property.

I like that. And not just because it's the law.

A house is a huge purchase. If you know the roof leaks, you really owe it to the buyers to let them know.

There's an important part, though, and it sounds like a loophole, but it really isn't. If you don't know, you don't have to disclose. In other words, if you heard that the roof leaks but you've seen no evidence of leaking, you don't have to say anything.

Why it's a good thing is because the buyers are going to find out anyway.

Sure, there are people who can sleep at night knowing they screwed somebody over. But I have to believe most of them sleep

Maybe it's just me, but I have this thing about relationships being built on mutual trust.

But even if you don't, here's why you need to be sure your partner knows everything. Because something is going to go wrong. And the thing that goes wrong is more than likely not the thing you think it's going to be.

better when they don't.

There's also a practical reason. If you don't disclose a material flaw that you knew about, there's a pretty good chance you're going to end up in court. Not only that, but there's a pretty good chance I'm going to end up in court, too.

Purchasing

<u>Rule #46</u>
Start with an Overview of the Market

Is $300,000 a screaming deal for a house? Is $200,000 stupid expensive? The only way to know the answer to those questions is to know what other houses like it go for.

Take a careful look at what's out there. And when I say a careful look, I mean more than just going by what people at work say or looking at the Zestimate™. If you're reading this book in order, you've already seen the bit about how a good real estate agent thoroughly evaluates the market in order to determine a reasonable price for a house. If your eyes glazed over, why don't you go back and read it again. It's Rules #9 and #10. Oh what the heck, as long as you're rereading, take another look at #15, too.

Go ahead. I'll wait here…

⇩

If you remember what I said in Rules #9 and #10, you know what I mean when I talk about the market.

Here's another thing that people do when it comes to real estate but are reluctant to do when it comes to love. Heterosexual people anyway. They don't check out their competition.

You know how hard it is to put up an online profile. It takes like 14 seconds.

Make another one, only this time be the opposite gender/sexual identity/whatever. Be the person you're looking to meet. Then use it to poke around and see who you're up against.

Women, you're going to be shocked to find that your prowess at parallel parking is not that unusual. And tacos. Apparently, women love tacos.

Men, you're going to be disappointed to learn that there are a lot of guys out there holding bigger fish and brandishing bigger pecs.

So? See what I'm saying?

The market determines value. Or to put it another way, what your house is worth depends on where it is.

Or to put it even another way, the three most important factors that determine what your place is worth are location, location, and location.

What makes this all kind of sad is that so many of those profiles that show and say exactly the same stuff? Those people invariably mention how unique they are.

Sigh!

Rule #47
The House You Want Isn't Going to Find Itself

Back in the old days, the general public didn't have access to real estate listings, so if you wanted to buy a house you had to engage the services of a real estate agent so they could share the homes available for purchase.

But the landscape has changed. If you're good at making a computer go, you have access to almost as much information as I do.

About listings.

Let me hasten to add that the landscape has changed in many other ways as well and if you bothered to read the footnote at the bottom of Rule #21, you realize that a real estate agent's job encompasses a lot more than opening a door and saying stuff like "good use of space." Especially as our society becomes more litigious and prices get higher.

⬇

Back in the old country there were matchmakers and actually, there still are in some cultures, but for the most part, people in our society are increasingly finding their own partners.

Is it a coincidence that our divorce rate is brutally high?

I'm not advocating for matchmaking. I mean, I see some real advantages, believe me. But no, I don't want someone else picking out my partner and I'm pretty sure you don't either.

It sure would be nice to have some guidance, though, wouldn't it? Like somebody ought to write a book on how to go about finding that person.

I mean, right?

Our job is increasingly about protecting our clients and unfortunately, when we do it well nobody notices. Well, until they hire the people who seduce them with a discounted commission and end up buying a house with a leaky roof and no recourse.

So it falls to you to find the place that you want to turn into your home. I can help. I can turn you on to neighborhoods you might not have considered, alert you to stuff that's coming onto the market, even come up with some crazy ideas that might work. And I can connect you with a ton of resources, from lenders to contractors, people I trust to do what they do imaginatively and ethically, so you can turn the home you want into the home you have and the home you have into the home you want it to be.

But first you have to find it and fall in love with it.

Rule #48
Pace Yourself

I know it's exciting, but there's a limit to how many houses you can see in a day without getting all fuzzy.

Here are a few tips that help:

- Keep notes on each house. Write them down as soon as you can after you see the place.

- Make up a catchy nickname that you can use with your broker (and partner, if you're buying together). It's a lot easier to not to lose track about which house you're discussing when you call one "Big Tree In Front Yard" instead of "6405 SE Fraser."

- If any home violates a single Deal Breaker (you did make that list, didn't you?) expunge it completely from your memory and your notes.

I know it's exciting, but there's a limit to how many people you can see in a day without getting all fuzzy.

Here are a few tips that help:

- Keep notes on each person. Write them down as soon as you can after you get together.

- Make up a catchy nickname that you can use to remember each person. (Important note: if you find yourself calling somebody "Smelly Guy" or "Too Much Makeup," that person probably didn't make an overall good impression. Just saying.)

- If any person violates a single Deal Breaker (you did make that list, didn't you?) expunge them completely from your memory and your notes.

- If you find yourself asking, "Was she the one with the nice laugh?" or "Was he the one with the beautiful smile?" you're seeing too many people at a time and/or you're not taking thorough enough notes.

- If you find yourself asking, "Was that the one with the green tile in the kitchen?" you're seeing too many houses in a day and/or you're not taking thorough enough notes.

Rule #49

If You're Looking Toward the Left It's Going to Come From the Right

I'm about to go all new age on you, but trust me, it works this way. Somehow, and I don't know how, the energy of looking for a thing makes the thing you're looking for show up. However, it usually doesn't show up where you're looking.

I know. Totally weird.

If you're dead set on finding a blue house on a corner lot, you're going to find a green house on a flag lot. But it's going to be the right house.

I think it might have something to do with making yourself receptive. Or maybe the universe listens, but has a sense of humor.

Aw, hell. What do I know?

When I'm on seven different dating sites, going out on three first dates a week, there's nothing. Not a spark. And then one day my neighbor's friend's daughter comes by and helps me figure out what's eating my azalea bush and the air practically crackles with electricity.

What I'm saying is that when you're not looking, you're not going to find it. And when you are looking, you're not going to find it where you're looking.

Rule #50
Every House Has a Center

Here I go again, getting all spiritual and shit, but it can't be helped.

When you go into a house, wander around and find the place you keep coming back to. Not the spot with the nicest view or the most comfortable place to sit. The place where you find yourself gravitating to.

That's the center.

Every house has one and honestly, I can't tell you why it's important. It just feels important.

I think it has to do with knowing a place. If you believe places have energy, it's where the energy emanates from. And if you don't, it's the place where the energy emanates from.

In a weird way, it's sort of the core identity of the house.

⬇

Here I go again, getting all spiritual and shit, but it can't be helped.

Take some time to go all introspecty. Yeah, that whole list exercise should have given you a good start, but this time, go all the way to your core.

Think about your foundational beliefs — about yourself, about others, about life.

Me, for example. I don't believe in limitations. I believe I can accomplish anything I set my mind to (in spite of, if I'm really being honest, several times when that turned out not to be true). I also happen to be an optimist, which kind of goes hand-in-hand with that other belief.

I believe most people are fundamentally good and that unless they're motivated by some need, like to protect their families, that they'll choose to do the right thing as long as it's not too difficult. I

Aw, hell. I don't know what the hell I'm talking about. It's just one of those cool things, that's all.

believe that all people should be treated equally and along with that,

all people should be held to the same level of responsibility.

I think I'm pretty smart, but that some people are smarter. I

think of myself as funny, but I'm funnier on paper than I am in person.

I admire people who are organized because I struggle with

organization. I'm not great at planning things in advance and I'm lazy

when it comes to doing research.

I like helping others. It's just the way I'm wired. More

specifically, I like helping others who have unrealized potential. But I

have very little patience for people who aren't willing to help

themselves.

Some of that stuff is going to sound pretty standard. Don't we

all believe that everyone deserves to be treated equally, for instance?

Well, it turns out that no, we don't all.

I know people who honestly believe they deserve preferential

treatment. And I know people who honestly believe they deserve to

get the short end of the stick. I know people who value poverty as a virtue, others who think that the standards they use to evaluate others should not be applied to them.

My point is, find your center. And then, every time you meet a new person, take a moment — take several moments — to set aside that list I keep harping on about and take the person in.

As a matter of fact, forget the list, at least as long as you're with the person. The questions to ask yourself when you're with someone are, "what does this person believe about themself?" and "what is this person's relationship to the world? and "how does this person make me feel?"

The reason this is important is that the stuff about you will often fit with stuff about someone else.

Sometimes you'll recognize patterns. That thing about helping people? Turns out, every relationship I had was defined by that. Sometimes, like in the case of the woman who I lived with for six-

and-a-half years, I didn't really need to help much. She was ambitious, determined, and diligent. She would have become an extraordinary success even if I hadn't done what little I did to help her along. Other times, like in the case of my ex, she was missing a crucial piece. She didn't believe in herself the way I believed in her. No matter how much I was willing to sacrifice my own career to help her out, she managed to choke. She just couldn't pull it off.

Once I recognized the pattern, I was able to do two things. The first was to see just how much a role it played in my desire for a relationship with someone. The second was to help identify the other person's patterns, priorities, and expectations.

In other words, how well connected my center would be to hers.

I've dated some extraordinary women since my divorce and I'm proud to say several of them have become really dear friends. Those friends are almost entirely everything on my list. They certainly meet every single Deal Breaker — I wouldn't bother spending time with

them if they didn't. But the reason those aren't romantic, long-term relationships is because their center and mine aren't entirely in sync.

I sound like a real asshole, don't I?

I'm not. Not really. I'm just particular. And I want whoever I end up with to be just as particular.

Rule #51

You Can't Step into the Same River Twice

If you've been paying attention, you noticed that this is the same as Rule #15, but because it applies equally to sellers as it does to buyers I'm putting it here, too.

According to a study by Redfin, Portland has about half a million single family homes.

And right now, 1,630 of those are for sale.

A year ago, there were 2,682 homes for sale. I can't give you an exact figure, but I guarantee you that the vast majority of those were not the same homes that were for sale a year later.

Just about 2,682 people found people to buy their homes. At a price — and with conditions — that made the deal worthwhile.

⇩

In 2017, the population of Portland was 647,805. There's no direct way to tell how many of those people were in relationships, but according to (https://www.bestplaces.net/compare-cities/portland_or/san_diego_ca/people), 56.9% of the population is single.

Even if 1/2 of those identify as a gender you aren't attracted to and 1/2 of the ones remaining are not attracted to people of your gender identity and 90% of the remaining people are either too young or too old for you, your odds of finding love are more than five times better than they are of finding a house.

That's kind of reassuring, isn't it?

And you know what? A year from now, the numbers will probably be pretty much the same. But the people won't be. A lot of folks will get married or move in together. And a lot of people will get divorced, split up, or kill each other. Same river, only totally different.

A lot of people who are single today will be in relationships in a year. A lot of people in relationships now will be single in a year.

If they hadn't, those houses would still be for sale. And instead of the number being 1,630, the number of homes for sale would be closer to 4,300.

We know those are different homes. How? Because the average Days On Market in Portland is 54. The average home is for sale for 54 days before it's sold. That's the average. The lowest possible number is either zero or one, depending on how you do the math, which means that for every house that's on the market for zero or one day, another house is on the market for 108.

To put that in not-math terms, for every home that gets sold the instant it's listed, another house sits unsold for less than a third of a year.

Which means that for a house to be on the market more than a year, more than three houses have to sell instantly.

See my point? Same river. But totally different river.

Same river, different river.

Rule #52

If the Home You're in Love with Falls Through, a Better One Will Come Along

When my then-wife and I moved to Portland, we found a really nice house in a charming area. Okay, sure, it was on the other side of the main street from where the cool shops were. And yeah, the apartment building two doors down loomed over it. And we had to talk ourselves into accepting the fact that you had to go through one bedroom to get to the other.

But we loved it.

And then the deal fell apart. And we were disconsolate. Someone told us to breathe. And that another better house would turn up.

Sure enough, the next day it did. Better area, prettier house, with three bedrooms instead of two.

⬇

Okay, I can't honestly tell you that I've experienced this one. My ex, though. She told me our marriage was dead and before the body was even cold she was introducing the kids to some other guy.

My kids tell me that all he did was criticize her and demean her. He complained about her cooking, which is hilarious because in the ten years we were married, she rarely cooked, but she did contribute a lot of expert opinion about the stuff I made.

Apparently, he did shit like let the kids go to the park unsupervised when they were six and seven, too. Oh, and he lied to her and cheated on her.

So yeah, in her case it worked out. She got someone who shared her values a lot more than I did.

So I think this rule holds.

That's one example and seriously, can you generalize from that?

Actually, yes.

I've seen it happen with clients. To put it a different way, I've never seen it not happen with clients.

Wanting to Spend the Night Somewhere Isn't the Same Thing as Wanting to Live There

My daughter had a rough year when she was 11. Her brother is autistic and thanks to a particularly boneheaded move my ex made, he spun totally out of control at school. The special needs team recognized the fundamental cause but didn't know how to handle it. Ultimately, he got traumatized by the very stuff the school was trying to do to fix the situation and because he often expresses himself in ways that aren't conventional, he was ostracized as a behavior problem.

Ultimately, he missed something like two and a half months of school. My ex and I homeschooled him during that time, which meant my daughter didn't get the attention he did. And when he went back to school, everybody — me, the school, and my ex — put so much

⇩

234

That list again.

Remember that third section — What I'm Attracted To — that's there to help you keep your eye on the ball.

Yes, that new receptionist in HR is smokin' hot. But are they you? Do they truly suit your lifestyle or are you going to have to make compromises in the things you value in order to live there?

Go back to Rule #50, the one about your center and theirs. If your centers aren't in alignment, go ahead and have fun. Just be clear with both yourself and the other person that it's not a recipe for a long-term relationship.

energy into helping him reintegrate that my daughter was left to her own devices.

For her part, she rose to the challenge. My daughter is an extraordinary student. She dedicated herself to school, doing her homework first thing when she came home and reading when there wasn't homework to do. She loves the Rick Riordan books (total digression, but it's interesting that not only are his protagonists often special-needs kids, but his own son is autistic) and she read and reread the novels so much that she became an expert on mythology.

She put her head down in every other way, but it didn't take a genius to see that she was suffering. It wasn't fair.

Add to that the fact that my ex had spent the first six years of our divorce dedicated to marginalizing me from the kids, and you can see why I decided that once things had settled with the boy, I needed to turn my attention to the girl.

So I planned a trip. Just her and me. I wanted to show her how

much I appreciated her and I wanted to be sure that our time together wouldn't be interrupted by a real or imagined need to pay attention to anything other than her.

Because she was into Greek mythology, I took her to Greece.

Greece is beautiful. The people are super nice. The food was amazing. We felt nothing but welcome wherever we went and we went places that would make your jaw drop they were so gorgeous. I wish we had more time. I would go back in a heartbeat.

But I don't want to live there. For one thing, my kids are in Portland. For another, I have a life, friends, career, dog, patterns… I love Greek food, but could I eat it every day? Could I live without pizza like they make at Char or the pho from the place down the street?

Greece is wonderful, but it doesn't suit my life. For me it's a place to vacation, not to live.

Do you see what I'm saying here?

Remember back to that list I told you to put together? That third section — What I'm Attracted To — that's there to help you keep your eye on the ball.

Yes, that mid-century modern house is beautiful. But is it you? Does it truly suit your lifestyle or are you going to have to make compromises in the things you value in order to live there?

Rule #54
Don't Buy for Resale Value

Real estate is an amazing investment. When you understand the power of leverage, you can see how so many people have accumulated serious wealth just by owning homes.

We real estate agents like to bandy that about as an incentive to buy a home, but I'm here to tell you that it's really a byproduct. Buy a home. A place to live. A place where you feel comfortable and safe.

If, as is extremely likely, after 30 years you find yourself sitting on a nest egg of massive proportions, awesome. But even if you don't, you'll have had 30 years of living in a place where you feel comfortable and safe. Where you don't need anybody's permission to paint a wall or even tear it out. Where nobody is going to make you move. Where you know exactly what it's going to cost to live there (mostly, but you know what I mean). Where you're not paying for somebody else to benefit from any appreciation that the property may have.

I'm sensitive to this because it's exactly what my ex did with me. I'm sure she thought I was relatively attractive, funny, attentive, and kind. But let's be honest. The reason she married me was because she saw the future. Or thought she did.

I was on a trajectory. I'd just finished a short film that was doing quite well in film festivals. I had an agent and a manager and was bringing in lots of money directing commercials for McDonald's. She had every reason to imagine that she'd be attending the Oscars in a few years and maybe even smiling as I accepted a trophy.

But it didn't work out that way and in no small part because it wasn't what I decided I wanted. I fell out of love with Hollywood. I didn't like the process. The work I was already getting was a slog and I extrapolated that if a 30-second commercial was often unbearable to work on, I could only imagine what it would be like to work on a 90-minute film.

So I took a detour.

Where it's yours.

And the woman I married felt betrayed.

She never said as much and I never asked. I figured that, like me, she was in it "for better or for worse."

She was buying for the resale value.

When it became apparent that the resale value wasn't there, she didn't see the value in having a place to come home to that made her feel safe and comfortable. Oh well.

Make Sure You Understand About HOAs and Other Assessments

An HOA is a Home Owners Association. Condos have them. Townhouses sometimes do. Detached single-family homes usually don't. When you live in a building with an HOA, you'll be assessed a certain amount, usually monthly. It's like additional rent, on top of your mortgage.

An HOA does a lot of important things:

• It's responsible for maintaining the common areas. If you live in a condominium, that means the exteriors, the walkways, the lavish gardens, the pools, the gym, the screening room, the community meeting rooms, and all that.

• It has the authority to establish rules. Some HOAs can be really strict. You can only paint your unit certain colors, you aren't

⇩

When multiple homeowners join together to set standards and make rules, that's an HOA. So think of a relationship as the same thing. Its own entity. One that's separate from, but intimately connected to, its constituent members.

Just like with an HOA, it's the responsibility of the relationship to maintain the common areas. It's the responsibility of the relationship to establish rules that govern all the "homeowners." And the relationship determines what reserves need to be maintained to cover repairs and maintenance.

And just like with an HOA, every person who's in the relationship is eligible to have a voice in the HOA business. When you establish your relationship, it's important to determine how much a voice each of the members has in the business of the HOA.

Since it's an organization of two, that means if you defer, the other person has complete authority. If you want complete authority, the other person needs to defer.

allowed to smoke in the building, stuff like that.

• It is legally required to maintain reserves that it uses for paying taxes, making major repairs, and performing regular and irregular maintenance. This is a big one that a lot of people misunderstand. Buildings need to be painted. The HOA will determine how often the building needs to be painted, hire the people to do the work, and take responsibility for ensuring that it's done properly. Painting is expensive. And when homeowners see that it costs, say, $275,000 to paint the building, a lot of the time they freak out. But it's important to keep in mind that this is the whole building that's being painted. Painting a house can cost $10,000. The reality is that (usually) it's cheaper to paint the whole thing than to paint all the individual bits separately. Another important point is that the HOA is legally required not to hire your nephew and his two buddies to paint the place. They're going to hire licensed professionals, based on the belief that licensed professionals A) know what they're doing, B) do

⇩

Work it out.

Some of this stuff will fall into place all by itself. If you're better with money, you might be the one who does the taxes. If it's more important to you that the counters are cleared, you might be the one it falls to to keep the kitchen clean.

professional quality work, C) are actually going to finish the job they start, and D) have insurance that covers everything from accidentally trampling your clematis to falling off a scaffolding and breaking a neck.

It's usually the reserves that freak people out. It seems like a lot of money. And it is. What a lot of people don't take into consideration is that whether you're in a house or a condo, you're going to have to maintain your property. It's going to have to be painted. An HOA sets aside money in advance to cover those things. Most homeowners don't.

When you buy into a condo, you'll be notified about HOA meetings. And generally, you'll be eligible to serve on the HOA board. So if you want to have a voice regarding what's done and how, you can.

Spouse Hunting: Using The Rules Of Real Estate To Find The Love Of Your Life

Rule #56
People Use Logic to Justify Emotional Decisions

As I write this, Apple has just introduced a new iPhone. It's pretty much the same as the old iPhone and once again, "experts" are maligning it as inferior to so many other phones out there.

This year, Apple also introduced a credit card. "Experts" climbed all over each other to weigh in on why the card was destined to fail because it didn't have any features superior to credit cards that are already available.

I'm going to go out on a limb here and say that not only will the new iPhone be a resounding success, the Apple credit card is going to redefine the entire credit card space. Why? Because the one thing that Apple is astonishingly good at is making an emotional connection to its customers.

People who buy Apple products aren't looking for megapixels

⇩

The story is so much a part of our cultural discourse that it's a cliché: A woman marries a man who beats her, but justifies it by explaining to her friends that " he's troubled." Admit it, you know at least one situation exactly like this. I know I do.

I believe that love is a biological mechanism. That eons of evolution have created in us a device that helps to ensure that people pair-bond. The benefit is that (from a strictly heterosexual point of view) females — who tended to be vulnerable to being eaten by saber tooth whatevers, especially during the time that they're pregnant and raising young nippers — could rely on a male to feed and protect them while males — who had a selfish motivation to see their genetic line continued — could rely on someone to raise young nippers to the point that they could go off and create a new generation.

Okay, I'm no Richard Dawkins. But it makes sense to me.

In our modern American society, women have less (some would argue no) need to be protected while men have no practical need to

⇩

or gigabytes or lumens. They're looking for Apple. When pressed, they'll justify their purchase by telling you how wonderful the features are and those of you who are like my brother will pounce on those arguments, swatting each and every one down with an example of a competitor's product that has more of whatever those things are. And then they'll scratch their heads, incredulous that they couldn't convince the Apple customer to change their mind. "You just don't get it," they invariably say. And I say back, "You're the one who just doesn't get it."

I use Apple because it's such a pure example. For having made inferior phones for so long, it's astonishing to note that not only has Apple become a bigger company than (almost) any other on the planet, ever, it does so at a PE multiple that's a fraction of its competitors and by the way, it's pretty much the only company in the entire space in which it competes that actually makes a profit. An extraordinary profit at that.

delegate the raising of their spawn to others. We've also come to a

point where the possible pair-bonding combinations go way beyond

"one man and one woman." But that societal progress hasn't had time

to develop a commensurate evolutionary change, so even if you're a

trans woman looking for a bi woman to form a partnership with and

have no desire ever to have kids, you're still working with wiring that

was developed before non-heterosexual relationships could possibly

have affected evolution.

So what do you do?

You limit your exposure. If you only encounter people who are

likely to be a good fit, when you do fall in love it's probably going to

be with someone who is actually going to be a good fit.

Wow. I went off on a rant there, didn't I?

But having worked extensively in automotive marketing, I can tell you that the same process goes on there. Lexus is Toyota. Infiniti is Nissan. Audi is Volkswagen. When I say "is" I'm not being figurative. Those car marques are little more than variations of the larger, more pedestrian brands, and the manufacturing is only distinct in some of the superficial materials used and the logos that get slapped on the cars. And yet. Do you know a single person who would prefer to drive a Toyota than a Lexus?

What does this have to do with buying a house?

Here's how it works: 1) you fall in love with a house, 2) you justify why that house is the one for you because of its bedrooms/bathrooms/proximity to good schools/etc.

When I say you, I mean we. We all do this.

I'm not advocating for trying not to do this. I don't think that's possible. What I do think is possible is to limit the houses you see to the ones that actually suit you. That way when you do fall in love with one, it won't be one that doesn't suit you.

Rule #57

Are You Looking for a Home or a Project?

There's nothing wrong with buying a fixer-upper. You just need to be clear with yourself that that's what you're doing.

Yes, you'll spend less than you would for an equivalent move-in ready house in the same neighborhood. A lot less. The basic rule of thumb that I go by is that if you double the cost of repairs and add it to the price, that will get you to what a move-in ready home would sell for.

There's another way to look at exactly the same formula. That you're going to spend money and time bringing the house up to the point where it's equivalent to other homes.

I've bought fixer-uppers and I'll tell you it's a lot of fun to bring a home back or to turn it into something special. But it always takes longer and costs more than you think it's going to. You have to be prepared for that.

People are different from homes in a very important way. When you take on that project — when you help a person become a more complete version of themself than they currently are — the person is at a new present.

What that means is that they're no longer who they were.

If you're looking for a partner you can help fulfill their potential, don't lose sight of your own potential. Work on yourself even more than you help them work on theirs. Because they may be incredibly grateful for everything you did, but there's a good chance they're going to evaluate you not as they did when you met, but as they are now.

Also, if you're looking for a partner who will help you become what you can be, please give a lot of thought to who you will be when they're done. Will they miss having a project? Will you miss being one? Or what if you never actually become what either you or that other person think you have the potential to be?

⇩

I'm not saying don't ever. I am saying that for most people, it makes a ton more sense to work on yourself first, then meet the person who appreciates you for who you are already.

Rule #58

Don't Fall for a Fresh Coat of Paint

It's amazing how visual people are. We fall in love with images. In fact, I'm surprised you're actually reading this book. You know nobody else is, right? They're all waiting for the Infographic version to come out.

There's a rule in real estate that you shouldn't paint your house with bold colors. Stick with off-white, the experts say.

I see it as half a rule. The whole rule is, "Don't paint your house with bold colors unless you know what you're doing."

Buyers are buying into a lifestyle. An image. If you don't know how to create that, then it's better to make sure your house is a clean slate. People can visualize a painting on a clean slate better than they can visualize removing the painting that's there and putting another one in its place. Mixing metaphors, but you know what I mean.

⇩

I hope you never have the opportunity to meet my ex-wife, but if you do, take a close look.

At first glance she looks flawless. And to be fair, she was blessed with a beautiful smile and great skin. She's also funny, pretty smart, and comes across as generous.

So you can understand why I fell for her.

When I met her she was working as a makeup artist. I didn't connect the dots. Of course she knew how to make her smile more glorious and her skin look flawless. And while those two things are superficial, they're also metaphorical. She said and did a lot of things that gave me an impression. So much so that even when the reality reared its ugly head, I was unwilling to believe that what I saw.

I saw only what I wanted to see.

You know that Maya Angelou quote? "When someone shows you who they are, believe them the first time?"

Yeah. That. Didn't.

The implication here is that when you're a buyer, make sure you're not falling for the fabrication. Look past the colors, the stylish furniture, the subtle scents that make a home so alluring. I mean, yeah, take them as ideas. They'll give you a good sense of what a home could be. But it's the structural stuff that tells you what a home is.

Once you buy a house, you can always hire an interior decorator to make it look the way you want. Or even the way you can't imagine. But if the foundation is crumbling, it doesn't matter how spiffy the dining room looks.

Rule #59

If the Paint Color Changes From One Listing Photo to Another, Be Cautious

Every once in a while you'll come across a listing where the photos don't quite match up. Maybe it's the paint color. Maybe the furniture is different.

What that usually means is that the pictures were taken at very different times and when you see that, you need to ask yourself why.

I mean, they got a photographer to come out and shoot the kitchen, the bedrooms, and the bathroom, but they decided that the old shot of the living room looked better? Hmmm.

Maybe it doesn't have anything to do with a water stain that developed on the ceiling. Then again, maybe it does.

I see this on dating sites all the time. Some woman will have short, blonde hair in one photo, long, brown hair in another. Or she'll be 45 pounds heavier in one.

What's that telling you?

It could be that, like me, the person doesn't like having their picture taken. And that's fair, but remember, you're on a dating site because you're making an official statement proclaiming to the world that you are actively pursuing a partner (Rule #23). So sure, even if you don't like having your picture taken, if a partner is something you're dedicated to achieving, wouldn't it behoove you to put a little effort into it? Yes it would.

So when somebody isn't willing to go to the trouble to have a picture or two taken, how seriously are they pursuing a partner? Probably not so much.

Of course, there's another side of this, too. Sometimes, you'll see a series of pictures where the person is wearing the exact same

outfit in every one, all the pictures shot in the same location at what appears to be the same time.

That's better, but not better enough. That's someone acknowledging that they need to present themself visually, but falling short of doing a complete job of it.

Look at the pictures. But go deeper than just the smile or the body. Examine where the pictures were taken and when. You can learn a lot.

Rule #60
You Can't Always Get What You Want

But if you try sometimes, you just might find you get what you need.

You want a mansion. One with a pool and a five-car garage and tennis courts and a screening room. While we're at it, let's throw in a mini planetarium.

Well, forget it.

The thing about love, it's a two-way street. You want to find the love who will love you back.

Yeah, it's possible that that might be Hugh Jackman or Jessica Alba and if it is, I promise I'll refund every penny you paid for this book, especially if you introduce me to Hugh. He seems like a pretty cool guy.

Anyway. Yeah, it's possible. I'm pretty sure it isn't going to happen.

Sorry.

Rule #61
See the Place at Different Times

There are times that a house makes a better impression. Like when the lawn has just been mowed. And there are times when a house makes a worse impression. Like when the motorcycle gang down the street practices doing wheelies out front. As a real estate agent, I make it a point to figure out when the house I'm listing is going to make the best possible impression and show it during those times.

Also as a real estate agent, I make it a point to figure out when the house my clients are considering buying is going make the worst possible impression and encourage them to see it during those times as well.

When I used to work with models, there was this weird thing that happened. None of them would show up for a casting session before 11:00 a.m. And they're models, so each one would look more amazing than the next.

I'd cast the best one for the part and then, because we want to shoot when the light is the best, we'd schedule them to be on set before dawn.

This wasn't a recipe for success.

I use this example to make a point. It goes way beyond looks. And it goes way beyond time of day. Someone who's happy during the summer can be miserable during the winter. Almost everybody is stressed around April 15th. The holidays can bring out all sorts of things.

Before you commit to a long-term relationship with someone, do yourself a favor and get a sense of what you're committing to. Know someone for at least a year. And pay attention.

Rule #62
Keep Your Commute to a Minimum

I used to live in LA. I saw tons of houses where the people who spent the most time in them were the housekeepers, gardeners, and nannies. The people who owned them were either working or, more likely, on their way to and from work.

We all have to work. Some of us are lucky and we can work from home. Everybody else has to get from home to work and from work to home and if you added up the hours you spend on the road and compared them to the waking hours you spend in your house, you might get really sad.

In LA, that's how a lot of people justify getting a nice car. It's where they spend their time. But I tell you what. I had a job once where I figured out how I could live a block and a half away. That was kind of awesome.

⇩

I don't believe in long-distance relationships. Maybe it's just me, but I want to be with someone I can share my day-to-day life with.

That being said, maybe you want a relationship that's more sporadic. Maybe you want to partner with someone who lives 3,000 miles away and who you only see once a month.

That's fine. The rule still holds and what I mean by that is that the commute is the thing that keeps you from the thing you want.

With a house, it's the travel time you have to endure in order to get from the thing you have to do (work) from the place you want to be (home). With a person, it's maybe not physical.

Back when I was young and stupid and living in San Diego I had a girlfriend who was equally young and stupid. I was ambitious in my career and when an opportunity came up for me to be in LA, I took it. Her job kept her in San Diego and so even though we'd

Now I know, there's a trade-off. Location, location, location. For the price of a one-bedroom shack near work, you can get a McMansion 45 miles out. I'm not saying to get a place next to the office at any cost. What I'm saying is that your commuting time is a cost. Getting a 1,200 square-foot house is awesome, but only if you get to spend time in it. And not a 100 square-foot car.

professed our love for each other, we both moved forward in a situation that meant that every Friday, I'd leave work, get in the car, and brave Southern California traffic to make what sometimes turned out to be a four-hour drive to see her for the weekend.

That was the physical commute.

But on her part, when we did get together, she would often spend Friday afternoons shopping, looking for a gift to give me, so she could express how glad she was to see me. It was time she could have been with me.

That was an emotional commute. Or maybe it was a psychological ploy she used on herself to protect herself from committing more deeply. Whatever. Both what I did and what she did created a distance between the thing we had to do with the place we wanted to be. And ultimately, it didn't work out.

Rule #63
You Should be Excited to Invite Your Friends Over

You love your friends. You love your house. Why wouldn't you want your friends to see your house?

Yeah, if you're like me, it's kind of a mess. But if you're like me, your friends understand that you always have 17 projects going, from rewiring the light fixture in the upstairs bathroom to sorting the nuts and bolts and washers and nails that have finally taken over the entire work surface in the garage.

If your friends don't get that, you need new friends, not a new house.

On the other hand...

Your potential partner is someone you're probably in love with. Being in love is awesome, but there's a huge difference between in love and love.

In love is about the future. In love is when you hope that the person you're with will be the person you will come to have a satisfying relationship with. In love is a trick of biology. It's evolution's way of fooling us into thinking something is there when it might not be.

Love is about the present. It's acknowledging weaknesses, recognizing strengths, and committing to someone because you have evaluated both.

The hard part is telling in love from love. And one super good way to do that is to step back and see how this person fits in with the people we already love. Family. And friends.

⇩

Spouse Hunting: Using The Rules Of Real Estate To Find The Love Of Your Life

If you find yourself bowing out of friendly get-togethers, or feeling like you need to explain (or apologize for) your partner to the people they're going to interact with, you're in love.

You already love your friends. You already love your family. And like the song says, "Love means never having to say you're sorry."

Rule #64
Wherever You Live Becomes the Center of Your Universe

Think about your life now. You buy your groceries at the same store. You get pizza from that same place. You walk your dog in that same park.

Unless you're really not like most people, those things that you do on a daily basis are all close to where you live.

You know what's going on in the neighborhood and if the hardware store is having a sale on pink flamingoes, you're going to know about it.

That neighborhood is your neighborhood, and this is where it gets difficult. When you're considering moving into another neighborhood, you don't know those things. Your life hasn't been established there. So it feels foreign. Uncomfortable.

Trust me on this. Your new neighborhood will become your

Pretend for a minute that my brother is your brother.

Whenever you make plans with him, he's late. Not just 15 minutes late. Sometimes three hours late.

If you're anything like me, you love my brother. He's truly one of the best things about being alive. He dropped everything — and I mean everything — three times to come up to Portland and help me through a divorce so despicable, if you'd seen it presented as a subplot on *Dallas*, you would have said, "that's totally unbelievable."

But he's always late.

He's so consistently late that I've learned to tell him we're planning to get together at three o'clock when we're really planning to get together at six o'clock. I make adjustments. I make adjustments gladly because he's my brother and he's worth it.

The behavior I accept and even make accommodations for in my brother is totally unacceptable in a person I'm meeting for the first time, and that's my point. We all have stuff. Me, I'm like the kid

home. It'll take a while, but you'll get to know its quirks — like the lady who goes around in a bathrobe, carrying a shovel will come to replace the guy in the turban who roller-skates to whatever disco song is playing in his head. You'll learn which Chinese place has the best dim sum and where to get a great burger.

What's even more interesting, your old neighborhood will fade into foreign-ness. It will. Even if the same people running the same places are there, as the years go by they'll become less and less a part of your life.

Change is hard. And I'm not going to say change is good because lord knows, I've had bad change. We all have.

who, when his father gave him a pile of manure for his birthday in an attempt to disabuse him of his optimism, gleefully started digging into the shit, saying, "With all this poop, there's gotta be a pony in here!"

You might find that pretty annoying. But if I were in your life, you'd accept that as just the way I am. You'd make accommodations for it. And eventually it would be just the way things are.

Rule #65
Get All the Information You Can Before You Make an Offer

A little bit of sleuthing can tell you a lot. I'm not saying it's okay to root through someone's garbage can, but is there anything wrong with checking out the books on the bookshelf? No there isn't.

Public records are your first and best friend. You can learn who owns a property, how long they've owned it, who they own it with, how much the property taxes are, who they bought it from... all sorts of things.

So you're seeing this person. Things are going well. You're thinking you might want to commit.

Awesome.

Obviously, this person has introduced you to their friends. If not, you might want to reconsider the entire relationship.

If so, there's your first place to look for info.

By this point you've heard stories. Think about them. Do any themes come up?

Let me give you an example. My ex-wife's friends and family told me hilarious stories about my ex. Laugh to the point of tears stories. Stories that pretty much always came down to the same thing: how she would desert someone who was relying on her.

Ha ha ha! She even told those stories about herself.

That last rule? The one about how wherever you live becoming the center of your universe? That's what became the center of my

universe. I got into a relationship where I knew the other person would not be there for me. I made accommodations. I convinced myself that it was perfectly fine for the primary relationship in my life to be with a person who was utterly and completely unreliable.

That's what's called a flag. A big, red flag.

Rule #66
Know the Zoning and Covenants and Restrictions

Like it or not, other people and organizations have the legal authority to tell you what you can and can't do with a property, even though you own it. Zoning laws impose limits on how big a house can be, how close to the property lines, and other important stuff.

Covenants and restrictions can go as far as to tell you what color you're allowed to paint it, how tall your hedges are allowed to be, and whether or not you can have pets.

These things aren't necessarily good or bad. They just are. If you don't like having those kinds of limitations, by all means find a property somewhere where the zoning laws are more lax and where you aren't living in a community that imposes those limitations.

Think of children, family, and friends as the equivalent of zoning, covenants, and restrictions. You enter a relationship with a person, but their children, family, and friends limit some of what you can do. And vice versa.

Take me, for instance. I'm divorced with two kids. My title is clear. I've done the major repairs and there's no reason I'm not qualified to enter into a relationship. But because of my kids there are things I am unable to do. I can't move to another state. (Okay, I could. But I'm not going to.) I have my kids every Thursday. So if we start dating, we're not getting together on Thursdays. If we get into a relationship, my kids are going to be a factor in any decision that involves Thursdays, whether that means going out of town for a long weekend or attending your Tibetan singing bowl recitals.

Kids are probably the most restrictive, but pets count, too. I come with Milo (Best Puppy Ever™). If you're allergic to dogs, that's

going to be a problem. Not a big problem because Milo is mostly

poodle, so I'm pretty sure he's hypoallergenic.

But I love Milo and even though the person I partner with isn't

required to love him, too, she is required not to expect me to

compromise my love for him.

Making and Accepting Offers

The First Offer Is Usually the Best One

This is one of those rules of thumb. It just seems to happen that way. If you get an offer, you should probably take it. Bird in the hand thing.

Let me start this rule by saying that *The Princess Bride* is truly one of the greatest films ever made. And unless you're a complete idiot, you agree with me on that.

That having been cleared up, I don't believe in that whole true love thing. I don't believe that there's one perfect person for you. Or me.

I think each of us could partner with myriad other people. None of those partnerships will be perfect and one will work better in one way than another. The person who inspires your creativity, for instance, may not share your love for pizza.

I've had enough relationships and examined enough relationships that other people have to come to the conclusion that the biggest factor that determines the success of a relationship is the people's commitment to make it work. I've seen people who are opposite in their philosophies, their politics, and their lifestyles have successful, loving relationships.

And I've seen people who you would think were identical in all three not able to make it last more than a year.

The one thing that does matter is values. If you and your partner don't share values — specifically the value of the relationship — it ain't gunna last. Like the saying I just made up goes, "It takes two people to be married, but only one to be divorced."

So when you find someone who doesn't violate any of your Deal Breakers and who either meets all the things on your Must Have A Compensating Reason list or has a good compensating reason for, an offer should be forthcoming.

Don't wait to see if another, better offer comes in. Take it.

Yeah, you might do better.

But you probably won't.

Rule #68
You Don't Have to Sell

I come across a lot of people who are reluctant to list their homes because they're afraid they'll get offers for less than they want.

You're allowed to say no.

When you get an offer, you have three options: you can accept it, you can reject it, or you can counter it. The thing to keep in mind is that when you submit a counteroffer, you're actually rejecting the original offer.

In other words, Yes equals Yes, No equals No, and Maybe equals No, unless you want to do it my way.

Of course, when the buyer receives your counteroffer, they have the same three options: accept, reject, or counter. That's one of the ways negotiations are done, but I'll get to that in the next section.

Remember way back in Rule #28, when I said that when people respond to a profile, they're not deciding between Yes and No, they're deciding between Maybe and No?

That's important.

Until you have a Yes, the best you can have is a Maybe, and Maybe isn't a bad thing to have. What Maybe means is, "let's see if this can turn into a Yes."

You're not leading someone on if you agree to go on a date. You're not even leading someone on if you agree to go on a bunch of dates. What you're doing is exploring the possibility.

If you're convinced you two aren't on your way to a relationship, that's when you need to have two honest conversations. The first is with yourself. Ask yourself if you're okay with continuing on with someone you clearly don't believe you can commit to.

If the answer is yes, then it's only fair to have a second honest conversation with the person you're seeing — the one where you tell

them what you're thinking and ask them what they're thinking. Don't expect that person to know what you're thinking. And don't be surprised if you find out that they're thinking something different from what you're thinking.

That can be a really hard conversation to have, but I'll tell you a secret. The harder it is to have that conversation, the less likely it is that you two belong together.

Rule #69
Choose the Buyer Who Best Fits the Neighborhood

Let's say you've done all the negotiating you can and you're looking at two identical offers. First of all, congratulations!

But now comes the hard part. Which one do you pick?

You pick the people who will best fit in with the neighborhood.

I know what you're thinking. You're thinking, "But Brian, I hate my neighbors."

All the more reason.

You're not going to live there anymore. You're moving somewhere else.

If you don't sell the house to them, they're going to keep looking. And they might end up finding a house next door to the one you end up buying.

Also it's good karma.

When I say "neighborhood" in the context of love, I'm talking about your friends and family. The people you surround yourself with.

So if you find yourself in the position of having two equally qualified suitors, pick the one who gets along best with the people you get along best with.

Equally, if you're one of two equally qualified suitors for a person, don't get in the way of them choosing the person who best gets along with their friends and family. Even if that's not you. Especially if that's not you.

Sounds so obvious when I say it, doesn't it?

Rule #70
Read the Title Report

When you buy a house you get crap tons of paper and I know it's tempting to stick it in a file and promise yourself that you'll look at it later.

Don't do that.

Read everything that comes in. It's actually pretty understandable, most of it, but yeah, there's so much that it's easy for your eyes to glaze over.

After you make an offer and it's accepted, one of the pieces of paper you should get from the lender is the title report. And why it's important is that you can't buy a house unless the person selling it actually owns it.

That's why one of the first steps we do during a transaction is have the title company run what's called a title report. It tells you who owns the property. Almost as important, it tells you who may have

⇩

The title report on a house tells you if the person selling it is actually legally able to sell it and if there are any outstanding obligations that need to be satisfied before it's sold.

People have kind of the same thing. We have obligations and not all of them are to you.

Is your potential partner married? I'm not old-fashioned, but that's a no-go. Contrary to what my ex-wife believes, marriage is more than a relationship of convenience. It's actually a legal state and it comes with rights and responsibilities.

If you die, the person you're married to probably gets to inherit your assets. If you end up in the hospital, the person you're married to gets to make important decisions about whether to pull the plug and what treatments you receive.

You do not want to enter into an intimate relationship with someone who is legally obligated to have a more intimate relationship with someone else.

claim to the property.

If a contractor worked on the basement and didn't get paid, they can place a lien on the home. What that means is they have a right to it. A right that supersedes yours.

I won't ever let my clients buy a place that doesn't have a clean title.

I'm not an asshole. They can always want to buy a place that doesn't have a clean title, but the title needs to be cleaned up before they move ahead with the purchase.

I know what you're thinking. You're thinking, "Okay, Brian. What about kids?"

I'm glad you asked. Kids count as obligations and responsibilities, especially when they're not adults. I have kids and I don't believe that disqualifies me from having an intimate relationship. What it does, though, is require me to be clear about the extent of my responsibilities and obligations to anyone who wants to be my partner.

For what it's worth, whoever I end up partnering with probably has kids, too. I want to know that the person I'm getting into a relationship with understands how important my kids are to me.

The important part is that those lines are drawn clearly. That's why I wrote Rule #66. The one on Deeds, Covenants, and Restrictions.

Rule #71
Make the Sale Contingent

A contingency is a thing that has to happen before a sale closes. In real estate, contingencies come in lots of flavors:

A financing contingency means a lender has to actually be willing to finance the purchase. If you can't get a lender to put up the money, you aren't stuck with a house you can't afford.

An inspection contingency means you have the right to bring in experts to examine the property and determine stuff that might not be apparent. Where we live, radon is a big thing. I always recommend that my buyers inspect for radon. Always. I also recommend that they have the sewer and roof inspected and if the house is older than, say, 30 years, I suggest they have an expert take a look at the electrical system.

There are also a couple of contingencies that lenders and title companies are sticklers for. The appraisal contingency requires the

I mentioned way back in Rule #6 that what you're looking for here is two simultaneous transactions. You want to find a partner who simultaneously finds you. So that's the biggest and most important contingency. Don't ever ever ever get into a relationship with someone who isn't getting into a relationship with you.

Ever.

In other words, stay away from people who are married. And no, I don't care that it's a loveless marriage and that they're only staying together for the kids or that it's just a piece of paper. In the words of the previous rule, that person does not have clear title. Somebody else has a lien on the property, even if they promise they'll never exercise it.

If you're absolutely convinced that the person you found is The One, please please please make sure you have a Title Contingency in place. That means they have to be free and clear of any other relationship before they enter into one with you.

house to be worth at least what you've agreed to pay for it. The title contingency says you can't buy a house if the person selling it to you doesn't actually own it. And connected but slightly different is the clear title contingency that says nobody else can put a lien on the house — like a contractor who didn't get paid for the bathroom renovation.

Those are important, but the one you really, really, really don't want to miss is a purchase contingency. That's the one that makes it so that one transaction doesn't close until another transaction closes.

This is the big one, at least as far as this rule is concerned. You can't buy this house until and unless the house you're selling closes.

That way you're not stuck with two houses. (It can be structured the other way, too, so that you can't sell this house until you find another one to buy.)

Choosing which way to structure the contingency has a lot to do with the kind of market we're in, the uniqueness of the house we're

By the way, that doesn't mean kids. Kids always take priority.

selling, the uniqueness of the property we're looking for, and how

realistic my clients are about the prices of both.

Rule #72
You Get an Inspection Period —
Use It

When you buy a house (in Oregon, anyway), an inspection period is written into the contract. You can waive the right to have professionals inspect the home, but unless you're planning to tear the place down and build something on the land, I always advise my clients to do a thorough job of inspecting the place they want to buy.

The first inspection is the general inspection. This is where someone who knows a lot about all the systems of the house goes through and calls out problems that they see. What a lot of people don't realize, though, is that the inspector isn't going to move furniture, remove outlets, or open crawl space accesses that have been nailed shut. Their job is to inspect what they can see. Which means that a wily homeowner can, for instance, patch and paint floor joists that were damaged in a fire and the inspector will have no way of knowing that there might be a problem.

When you're thinking about partnering up with a person, that's when you have an inspection period. It's not formal like when you're buying a house, but it's every bit as important. You want to know what you're getting. And you want your potential partner to know what they're getting as well.

One super important thing. Well, two. The first is that during an inspection, stuff always comes up. Always. You're not perfect and neither is your potential partner. The second is that that's fine. Knowing the flaws and quirks isn't a bad thing. In fact, it's a good thing. After all, this is a person you're going to commit your life to. Like with a house, if you patch the charred floor joists and paint them so nobody can tell there's fire damage, you're actively hiding something from someone you ostensibly love.

You don't want to do that. And you sure as hell don't want them to do that to you.

The second part of the inspection period is the part where you

Of course, in Oregon homeowners are required to disclose any material fault that they're aware of. In my experience, most of them do. Also in my experience, some of them don't.

The general home inspection will often reveal stuff that deserves a closer look. The roof and the electrical system are two that come up a lot. So I make sure to write into the contract that the buyers have an option to do additional inspections recommended by the general home inspector.

Some things can't possibly be examined during the course of a general home inspection but usually deserve to be looked at. So I also recommend bringing in specialists to check the sewer system and to test for radon. There's more, but you get the idea.

make repairs. This is important. You're working on yourself. Your potential partner is working on themself.

You think you two could make more progress on yourselves if you were there to support each other.

Awesome.

Write it down.

I know, I sound like an asshole. I'm really not.

I'm not saying you need to have something to hold over your partner, like some performance clause or something. But what I do think is that it's a good idea for both people to understand where their limitations are.

Relationships are hard. It works when you're both supportive. It's supportive to be clear, isn't it?

Rule #73
The Property Has to Appraise

One of the fun parts of my job is figuring out what a home is worth. I go to a lot of trouble, comparing it to similar properties not just in the same neighborhood, but in other similar neighborhoods. I factor in all sorts of stuff, like the gas station that's two blocks away or the way the living room floor slopes dramatically toward the kitchen.

Lenders, though, they don't care what I say. They refuse to underwrite a loan unless a licensed appraiser says the home is worth at least as much as the buyer and seller agree to for the purchase price.

This is a good thing.

I like to think I'm super ethical and I know a lot of the realtors I interact with are equally ethical, but that doesn't mean all realtors are. Especially these days when Zillow can spit out a number that's supposed to represent what your house is worth based on an algorithm

⇩

If only there were appraisers for relationships, huh?

Well, there are. They're called family and friends. They're going to give you an appraisal, but here's the hard part. They're probably going to be nice about it.

They love you. They don't want to hurt your feelings. So it's going to be up to you to read between the lines and ask for clarification.

and absolutely no local knowledge.

If you want to buy a house for $400,000 and the appraiser says it's worth $375,000, you have a problem.

You don't have to listen to the appraiser. But the bank will. If you decide that the appraiser is wrong, you can still buy the house. You just won't be able to finance all $400,000. In other words, you're put in the position of having to decide, really and truly, that the house you love is worth it.

Rule #74
Read the Contract

If you took my advice back in Rule #15, you hired a realtor to help you write up an offer.

If you didn't, you're an idiot. You probably downloaded a copy of the standard contract we work with and you're scratching your head, trying to figure out how to fill in the blanks.

Realtors are here to help you, but ultimately, the house you're buying is yours and the responsibility for the terms of the transaction falls to you.

Read the contract.

Sure, it's full of legal jargon. People like me can help translate it. And yeah, it might take you a while to get through it all. Trust me, that's time you really want to spend.

Know what you're getting into.

Marriage is a legal status and it comes with rights and responsibilities. Know them.

(An important caveat: A clever lawyer — like the one my ex-wife employed — can eliminate your responsibilities, maximize your rights, maximize your partner's obligations, and eliminate your partner's rights. Which is why you really want to pay attention to Rule #65 and partner up with someone whose moral compass points to the same north that yours does.)

Assuming you go into a relationship with someone whose values you share, make sure you're both clear on your rights and responsibilities. To each other. To yourselves. To others. You don't have to be married to do this. In fact, if you're not getting into a marriage, that's even more reason to have these things spelled out.

One of the huge disadvantages of a non-legally recognized partnership is that you can't presume that you share rights and responsibilities. If one of you dies, the other doesn't automatically

inherit. If one of you ends up in the intensive care unit, the other doesn't automatically get to have a say on treatment. Or even get to visit.

Think this shit through. You're partners. There needs to be a clear understanding of what that means exactly.

Negotiating

Rule #75

Find Out What's Important

As I write this, the median sale price for a home in Portland is $416,400. That's a lot of money. So yeah, the price is an important factor.

Also as I write this, 1,630 homes are for sale in Portland.

Put those two facts together and what you have is a situation where there's more than one home that a buyer can afford.

I can't find a number for the number of buyers, but we can interpolate. The average home in Portland is on the market for 67 days. Since it takes an average of 45 days to go from offer to closing, that means it takes the average home 12 days to get an acceptable offer. Add to that the average listing is $459,900 sale closes for $424,300, or about 7 1/2% less. What that tells me is that there's a pretty good balance between sellers and buyers or to put it another way, there are a lot of buyers for every home that's listed.

⇩

When you're looking to go under contract with someone, you need to know not just what your priorities are (Rule #4), but also what theirs are.

Most people will tell you, if you listen closely enough.

Here's a test. You've read enough of this book. What do you think is one of the most critical characteristics I'm looking for in a partner, thanks to my previous experience with my ex? I'm going to make this multiple choice so it's even easier:

[ ] A. That she's hot

[ ] B. That she's funny

[ ] C. That she has principles

[ ] D. That she's rich

You know the answer. If you don't, go back and reread the book. I'm serious. I told you what matters to me. Everybody does.

⬇

All of that is a long lead-up to an important point: Price matters. But other stuff matters, too.

Buyers can choose from among lots of houses at whatever price point, so they're going to put an offer on the one that makes them feel good. Sellers can sell to lots of buyers (as long as they price their home realistically), so they can choose the buyer who makes them feel good.

There's a corollary to this: You can't be special to every buyer or seller out there. But that's okay because you don't want to be. Remember *The Incredibles*? Here's a snatch of dialogue which expresses the theme of the movie perfectly:

```
Elastigirl: Everyone is special, Dash.

Dash: That's just another way of saying no one
is.
```

When you know what's important, you know how to get what you want by letting the other person in the negotiation have what they want (Rule #81).

That doesn't mean that both of you have to have the same things that are important. What it does mean is that if you don't have the characteristics your potential partner is looking for — AND your potential partner doesn't have the characteristics you're looking for — you'll be doing both of yourselves a favor if you walk away.

Oh look. Here comes another rule about exactly that.

Rule #76
Be Prepared to Walk

When you're negotiating a real estate transaction, you have two options. Make it work. Or don't.

Of course you want to make it work. But sometimes the party you're negotiating with is unwilling to let you have what's important to you. Or vice versa.

If it comes to that, be willing to walk away.

The willingness to walk away puts you in a powerful position, especially if the other party wants the deal to close more than you do. They'll have to decide whether to make the sacrifice you're asking for or lose the transaction completely.

Just remember, though, that you can't brandish a weapon unless you're absolutely willing to use it. If you threaten to walk, know that there's a very good chance that you'll have to.

I've heard it said that there's no such thing as a relationship that's truly equal. That one person always loves more than the other.

The person who loves more is at a disadvantage.

I'm not saying that you should love your partner less than your partner loves you. What I am saying is that if you come to realize that your potential partner is deficient in any characteristic that you have decided is important, you need to be prepared to say goodbye.

Trust me, the pain of leaving will be less than the pain of staying.

Be prepared to walk. It's the best way to protect yourself.

And that leads me to…

Rule #77
You Can't Read Minds

When I say "can't" I mean you don't have the ability, not that you're not allowed to. If you actually have the ability to read minds, go right ahead. But you don't.

So when you're tempted to say, "The buyers won't go for that," just shut your self up.

You don't know. You don't know until you ask.

You might be right. But you might be surprised.

The whole point of dating is to get to know someone. So until you do, resist the temptation to jump to conclusions.

A parable:

I had a girlfriend who used to put the toilet paper in the little holder thing with the paper coming out of the bottom. I like it coming out of the top. But she refused to see the wisdom of my approach and I refused to see the wisdom of hers. It got to the point that she would put the toilet paper on the thing the wrong way JUST TO PISS ME OFF.

And yeah, I admit. I did the same thing to her.

We broke up, for totally unrelated reasons, but the toilet paper wars didn't help.

Years later, I met someone pretty wonderful. The first time I used the bathroom at her place my eye went straight to the toilet paper. She put it on the wrong way. And I knew…

Only I didn't.

Spouse Hunting: Using The Rules Of Real Estate To Find The Love Of Your Life

338

I came out of the bathroom prepared to do battle. "So what's with the toilet paper," I asked, probably with a bit too much antagonism in my voice.

"I know!" she said. "Gladys (her cat) loves to unroll the toilet paper when I'm at work, so I have to put it on there upside down."

You don't know why somebody does something. At least not until you ask.

Ask.

Rule #78

Three Phases to Negotiating a Transaction

I'm kind of astonished how many realtors don't look at it this way, but when I'm working with a client, I approach the negotiations in three distinct phases.

Phase 1: Before the offer. If I'm working with a buyer, this is where I suss out how much interest there is and how motivated the seller is to sell. I float notions to see how much flexibility there is on price. I find out as much as I can about other factors that might be important to the people selling. When I'm working with a seller, I do the same things from the other point of view. How anxious are they to move? Are there other properties they're interested in? Any other factors that might affect how much they can or will spend?

Phase 2: This is the offer itself. If I've done a good job in Phase 1, I've moved the price up for the sellers or down for the buyers. But

⇩

Yep, just like when you're negotiating the sale of a home, entering into a partnership involves three distinct phases of negotiation.

Phase 1: This is dating. You present your best self and so does your potential partner. If the dating goes well it leads to...

Phase 2: The offer. In a conventional marriage relationship, this is the proposal. "'Tiffani, will you make me the happiest man in the world?" That's an offer. "You'll do." That's another offer.

Most of the time, the terms are implied and that's dangerous. I'm not saying that because I'm a lawyer because I'm not. I'm saying that because you may both think you understand the terms, but unless you set them forth, you don't.

If you're not into the institution of marriage and I get that because I'm not, there still needs to be a formalization of the relationship. The part where you give her your letter jacket and you officially start going steady. What too many people (including me)

now we have something concrete to move even further from (if possible).

The buyer writes up the offer and the seller responds. There are only three possible responses: Accept, Reject, or Counter. I usually advise my clients not to accept or reject. Because there's usually more we can get and concessions we can minimize.

Phase 3: The repair addendum. The inspections reveal stuff, usually not positive stuff, and as a result, the advantage is to the buyers at this point. When I'm working with sellers, I advise them to disclose everything — the fewer surprises, the less room there is for buyers to make demands. But it's not just the repairs that put the buyers in the advantageous position. Once a house is under contract, it's off the market. The sellers are still paying the mortgage, though. Plus utilities, insurance, and taxes. So if the transaction doesn't close, they lose a month or two of those expenses, only to have to start over.

If they have to relist the property, there's always a question

do is skip this step. They go from "hey, you seem awesome" to "we're a couple" without working out the terms they propose and without acknowledging that this is where they seriously pursue the notion of the relationship. In harsh terms, where they negotiate what the relationship is going to be if it's going to be.

Phase 3: The ceremony. This is where the couple agrees to final terms. "To have and to hold, in sickness and in health, for better or for worse, until death do you part." That's a contract. Those are boilerplate terms, but it's up to you to personalize them if it's appropriate to do so.

Also, and I'm only saying this because I married such a greedy, amoral narcissist: I'd recommend putting an enforcement mechanism on every single term.

Yeah, I have trust issues. Working on those.

about why the previous transaction didn't close. It's a taint that can

put your houses at a disadvantage. And if you're in a strong buyer's

market, the same buyer can come back in with a lower offer that

you'd be an idiot not to consider.

Rule #79
Be Smart About Negotiating Repairs

In Oregon, when you buy a house the contract specifically states that you're buying it "As Is." The contract also specifically states that you are entitled to an inspection period during which you can hire experts to find health and safety issues (well, any issues, really) that aren't apparent.

See where those two things are contradictory?

You can find out all sorts of stuff that's wrong, but you're saying that you want the house regardless.

The way those two are reconciled is with a clause that permits you, the buyer, to terminate the sale by expressing your unconditional disapproval of the state of the house, based on anything you like that comes to light during the inspection period. And that's where the window for negotiating repairs opens up.

⬇

You ever see those couples who, even though they've been married for years, one or both of them carry bitter resentment toward the other?

Most of the time it comes down to not having negotiated repairs before closing.

Take my mom, for instance. She and my dad have been married more than 60 years. And in all that time, he's never bought her a birthday present.

Why?

You'll have to ask him. The thing is, she didn't. Before they got married, she didn't say to him, "I'd like to marry you, but there are some things I want to fix."

And to be fair, I'm sure there's stuff about my mom that bugs my dad.

I know what you're thinking. You're thinking, "Brian, how can

I've seen Repair Addendums for crazy shit. Painting a bedroom.

Installing new windows. Removing a tree. The implicit threat is "do

this or I'll unconditionally disapprove of the condition of the house."

When it's a buyer's market, there's a lot of pressure to do those things

— or to reduce the price. After all, sellers want to sell the house.

When it's a seller's market, buyers are sometimes reluctant to even

call out legitimate stuff that they couldn't have been aware of prior to

an inspection — like dangerous wiring or a foundation that's

crumbling.

I possibly know all the things that are potentially going to bother me 60 years from now?"

You can't. And even if you did, like a house inspection it's not like you're going to ask for everything to get fixed. You're connecting with a person who's connecting with you. You're not going to be perfect, either one of you. But if there's something big, now's the time to bring it up.

But let's say you miss something. Something important, like birthday presents. Just because you don't address it during the inspection period doesn't mean you have to live with it. I'll get to that later, in Rule #96.

Ultimately, it comes down to who is more willing to walk away from the deal. You may not like it. You may be in the kind of market where you're at a disadvantage. But that's the way it is.

Rule #80

Talk to the Neighbors and the Previous Owners

Real estate agents like to impose themselves between the buyers and the sellers and there are good reasons for that. We keep things objective. We adhere to timelines and accepted practices. We're good at making sure agreements are clear, legal, and enforceable.

The hard part is that it can take a lot of the love out of an emotional decision.

I'm lucky. Most of the clients I work with are people I actually like. We share some something. And most of the people my clients buy from or sell to seem to be equally sympatico. So whenever it's appropriate, I like to put my clients in touch with the people they're entering into a transaction with.

Almost without fail, buyers I work with become incredibly invested in their neighborhoods. And sellers I work with stay in touch

⬇

You're not just entering into a relationship, you're entering into the relationships that the person you're partnering with already has. Those are the neighbors.

So you might want to make sure you get along.

If you don't get along, you might want to find out why.

with the people who buy their home — getting updates on the renovations they're making and how the tomatoes are coming in this year.

Rule #81
In a Good Negotiation
Everybody Wins

I hate the expression "win-win," but I have to admit it's a pretty succinct way of expressing the idea I want to get across here.

When you're selling your home, yes. You want to maximize your return. But every month that your house doesn't sell is a month that you have to make a mortgage payment on it.

When you're buying a home, yes. You want to minimize the cost. But every month that you go without buying is another month that you're living in the place you want to leave instead of the place you want to be.

Dollars are important. That's why you hire someone like me — to negotiate a deal that's going to make you happy. But life is more important.

I can't believe I'm this far into the book before I remembered to mention this, but why do you want a partner?

To be happy.

And why does a partner want you?

To be happy.

You both want the same thing. You can both have the same thing. All you have to do is keep that in mind.

<u>*Rule #82*</u>
Don't Be Afraid to Ask Questions

In order to get my real estate license, I had to take 150 hours of coursework and pass an exam.

After that, I had to get trained.

And after that, I'm required to do a bunch of continuing education.

None of this is stuff you couldn't do, but I bet it's stuff you didn't do. So I get that you don't know the difference between a mortgage and a trust deed. You're not expected to. I am.

That's one of the reasons you hire me. If you don't feel comfortable asking me a question — any question — about real estate, you need to fire me and work with somebody else. But I do my best to make sure that doesn't happen.

⇩

Love is harder than real estate in some ways because there's no such thing as a person who's trained to guide you into a successful relationship.

But love is easier than real estate in other ways. Because look around. Almost everybody has been in, or wants to be in, a relationship.

And since the laws don't get into the minutiae of relationships the way they get into the minutiae of real estate, people try all sorts of shit. And some of it works.

Even if it doesn't work, you can learn why it didn't.

All you gotta do is ask.

Trust me on this, people will be happy to tell you what works for them. They'll be even happier to tell you what doesn't.

Here's another thing. You may ask me a question that I don't know the answer to.

That doesn't make me a bad real estate agent. That makes me an honest one.

I don't know everything. For the very simple reason that there's so so so much to know.

What I do know is how to find out.

Closing

Rule #83
Make Sure the Transaction Closes

The goal when you're buying and/or selling a house is simple: to buy and/or sell a house. Not to hang out with a house and see where it goes.

And since there's a ton at stake, we have what's called a closing. It's the exact moment when ownership of the property officially changes hands.

It's important to have that moment. Not just for closure (hmmmm…. Is that where that comes from?), but for other reasons as well.

Property taxes and utilities, for example, are owed by the owners. An even bigger reason is insurance. If the house burns down at 4:22 p.m. and the change of ownership is recorded at 4:23 p.m., the sellers' insurance is on the hook. But if it burns down at 4:24 p.m., it falls on the buyers' insurance.

⬇

The most obvious analog to a real estate transaction closing in relationships is marriage.

I get it. You may not believe in marriage. You may live in a state where your partnership is not eligible to be consecrated.

It's still important to have a moment — an exact moment — that you officially became partners.

For one thing, it's important to acknowledge that you are partners. Both of you. Don't assume that because you feel like partners that the person you're with feels the same way.

For another, how are you going to celebrate an anniversary if you don't have a date to celebrate?

There's also legal crap. You get hit by a car, is your partner going to have the ability to visit you in the hospital? The authority to pull the plug? Inherit your shit?

And what happens if the fire breaks out at 4:15 p.m., but the house doesn't finish burning down until 6:23 p.m.? You and your insurance companies go to court, probably.

Spouse Hunting: Using The Rules Of Real Estate To Find The Love Of Your Life

Rule #84
Agree on a Timeline

People talk about the price of homes, but there are other parts to a transaction that are also important. The second biggest one is the timeline.

In real estate, there are limitations. For a lender to do an appraisal and fund, a title company to complete a title search, a pack of experts to do all their inspections, and buyers and sellers to negotiate repairs, it's generally at least a month between making an offer and closing. Legally, I don't think there's any limit, though, to how long an escrow can last.

I usually recommend between 30 and 60 days, depending on how quickly buyers and sellers want to move and whatever external factors might affect the transaction moving along.

Just because you've read this book, there's no telling that the person you meet and want to partner with has. Or will. So it may be one of those things where you decide on something, you take all the steps, and making it official seems like the logical next step.

Your partner may not feel that way. And that's cool. Just something you need to talk about. Get on the same page. This page.

I've found that the thing that fucks up more relationships than anything else is expectations that one person has about the other that the other isn't even aware of.

Closing the transaction is important. You know it is because I told you so in the last chapter. So work it out with your partner when it's going to close, how you're going to know that it's closed, and how you're going to celebrate.

Rule #85
Don't Let the Transaction Stall

Real estate transactions have momentum, or at least they should if you're working with a good realtor.

Part of that comes from the way compensation is structured in real estate. We don't get paid until the transaction closes, so we have an incentive to keep things moving.

Part of that also comes from experience. We know that if the transaction stops moving forward, like a shark it's likely to die.

So we set timetables and keep things moving. There are a lot of things to keep moving, too. Things you don't necessarily see when you're the buyer or the seller.

If you're in a transaction and you're not feeling that things are moving, check in with your agent right away. You should get immediate reassurance that things are happening. Constantly.

⬇

Remember that rule about committing to commit? When you commit to committing, you're establishing a goal. Every action you take should move you closer to that goal.

Every date should be about getting to know each other better. Which means that every date is an opportunity to evaluate the person under consideration.

Yes, that sounds sterile. It isn't. It's clear.

You need to find out how this person handles disappointment. What they think is fun. How they treat waiters. Whether they get along with children and dogs. You need to know what this person is like sick. Tired. Stressed. Happy. You need to see patterns — planning, improvising, making decisions, listening, cleaning up a mess they made, cleaning up a mess they didn't make.

All this is forward progress, at least as long as your potential partner doesn't exhibit behaviors that throw a questionable light on your future relationship.

If you check each other's boxes, then it's time to move to the next phase. If you don't, it's time to move on.

Either way, keep things moving.

Yes, it should be fun. But fun is not the goal. The goal is the partnership. Keep that in mind.

Spouse Hunting: Using The Rules Of Real Estate To Find The Love Of Your Life

Happily Ever After

<u>Rule #86</u>
Stop Looking

Buyer's Remorse is a real thing. Especially given the nature of home buying. There's a lot at stake, the process is stressful, and the home you end up with inevitably requires compromise.

Stop.

Just stop.

Look back at where you were when you started this process. Remember what you've been through. How hard it was to find something that you felt like you could turn into your home.

You did something really tremendous.

Now you get to be done.

You're done. You've followed the steps in this book and you've been honest with yourself. And look at you! You've found what you're looking for. Why would you want to keep looking?

Yeah, there will always be someone better looking, or funnier, or smarter. To be honest, there might actually be someone who's overall a better fit for you.

But even if there is, that person has to think you're a better fit for them. Plus they need to be ready to commit to a relationship with you.

The truth is, there's no such thing as perfect. And once you've found someone who meets all your needs and covers most of your wants, stop thinking and go for it. Because trust me, what you've found is rare.

Don't fuck it up.

Rule #87
You Can Only Have One Home

If you're well off, you can have several houses. But you can only have one home. One place where you feel truly comfortable.

If you spend any time on dating sites, you see plenty of people in "ethically non-monogamous" situations.

The ethical part involves having a primary. That's the partner.

It's impossible to have more than one primary. That's the definition of primary.

The corollary is that two is a partnership. Three is a committee.

Committees suck. They don't work.

Remember Jonestown? Waco? Utah?

You get one partner.

Seriously, you're lucky if you get even one.

Rule #88
Get a Home Warranty

I don't care if your home inspection said that everything was in perfect condition. I don't care if you bought a brand-new home. Get a home warranty.

I always try to negotiate for one as part of the sale. If you can't get someone else to spring for it, though, buy it yourself.

You never know what's going to go wrong, but I guarantee something will.

Roofs are expensive. Dishwashers are expensive. Water heaters are expensive.

It's not just the money, it's the hassle. Life is full of uncertainty, but the one thing we can rely on is that your furnace will go out on Christmas Eve.

Get a home warranty.

Now that you're partnering up with someone else, it's going to be tempting to continue just blithely going through life taking all sorts of risks. And that's a good thing. Hopefully, you'll be crossing streets, eating bacon, and engaging in all sorts of risky behavior with someone.

Someone it would suck to lose.

Make sure you both have health insurance. Make sure you both have life insurance, too. Especially if you start making babies.

The partner you worked so hard to find is irreplaceable, so yeah, no amount of money is going to compensate you for your loss. But It's better to lose someone and have a funeral paid for than lose someone and have to cough up thousands of dollars.

You're spending hundreds of thousands of dollars on a house.

You can afford to drop a couple hundred on a warranty.

Spouse Hunting: Using The Rules Of Real Estate To Find The Love Of Your Life

Rule #89
Put Up a Fence Before You Move In

Trust me, it's super awkward to go up to a neighbor after you've lived next door for a while and say, "Hey, I'm planning to put up a fence." Feelings get hurt.

Broach the subject early. Before you move in.

I recommend knocking on your new neighbor's door carrying a plate of cookies. Introduce yourself. Tell them how excited you are to move into the neighborhood. And mention that you'd like to put up a fence.

Feelings won't get hurt because you aren't friends yet. In fact, you might find that they'd like a fence, too, and that they're willing to help pay for it.

If you're not sure if you want a fence, get one anyway. If you end up being super good friends with your neighbor, do what we did:

Fences are boundaries between neighbors and in relationships, establishing boundaries is a good thing.

I happen to live in an amazing neighborhood. Milo (Best Puppy Ever™) loves to have any and all of the dogs in the neighborhood over for playdates and because of that my front yard is kind of a gathering place. I sometimes come home to five neighbors on the porch and six dogs chasing each other around the yard.

The neighbors I'm closest with know where I hide the key and they have no hesitation about letting themselves in to use the bathroom, find their dog, or help themselves to snacks. At one point some of my neighbors made a joke about eating the last of my barbecue potato chips and from then on, I always made sure to have at least two bags in the pantry for them.

I love living this way.

Whoever I end up partnering up with might not.

take out a section of the fence and put in a gate so the kids can go

back and forth between the two yards.

Remember that woman I lived with for six and a half years? We're still extremely close. When she needs help on a project, she'll often hire me to help. Sometimes that help requires travel. I've been to Chicago, New York, Atlanta, Austin, and Los Angeles with her.

I love living this way.

Whoever I end up partnering up with might not.

So if and when somebody new comes into my life, we're going to have a talk about this and other things we do with friends and neighbors and ex-partners. Both of us. And we're going to establish boundaries we can both be comfortable with.

I recommend you do the same.

And if you can't agree on what's cool, I recommend you do the more conservative thing. Put up the fence that makes the less comfortable partner feel safe.

You can always put in a gate later. It's a lot easier to put in a gate than to put in a fence.

Rule #90
Get to Know Your Neighbors Right Away

You're going to be living in a neighborhood and that means you're going to have neighbors. And since the average homeowner stays in the same house for more than 13 years, it only makes sense to get to know the neighbors.

Do it right away.

Go around and introduce yourself. Bring cookies.

Sometimes it won't work. I moved into a neighborhood once and took my kids around, with brownies, to meet all the neighbors. Who wouldn't want to say hello to the most adorable five- and six-year-old ever?

Apparently the people in this neighborhood, that's who. Most of them wouldn't even come to the door (and I knew they were home — I'd seen them park the car in the driveway from across the street). Needless to say, we didn't stay in that neighborhood very long.

Your partner comes with friends, family, and coworkers. These are the people who are already in their life and just because you show up, they're not going away.

Yes, you get to be the most important person in their life, but don't plan on being the only person.

Meet them. Respect their history. Let them have their inside jokes, their traditions, and their stories. You'll get yours eventually. But don't take theirs away. That's not just insecure, it's mean.

Rule #91

Don't Try to Turn the House Into Something It Isn't

Remember that list I made you put together? Of course you do. I won't stop bringing it up. Well, I'm bringing it up again and this time in the context of "you found the perfect home."

That third section of the list? The stuff you're attracted to? You're going to be tempted to turn your house into that.

Try not to.

I mean, sure. Paint. Decorate. But don't put Corinthian columns in a mid-century modern home.

Let the house be true to itself.

I had a girlfriend once who kept buying me new clothes. Really nice clothes. Clothes that were… shiny.

But I'm kind of a slob.

I mean, I don't go around in a sweat-stained wifebeater, but I'm really talented at spilling stuff on me. And I'm just about always working on something that can spill.

She was pretty awesome in so many ways, but that thing where she tried to make me what I wasn't comfortable being precipitated the breakup.

Don't do that.

That's not to say you shouldn't help your partner improve. But have the conversation first. Find out what your partner wants. Then by all means, help them achieve it.

Rule #92
If You Think You Got a Great Deal, You Did

I was doing a marketing project for a car company with my friend, the woman I lived with for six and a half years. We were in Austin, interviewing people who'd bought new pickup trucks from this particular company.

One of the men we interviewed was super-excited about the great deal he'd gotten on his truck.

We asked how he knew. Did he research prices? Did he shop competitive vehicles? Did he come to the negotiation armed with facts and figures?

No. None of that.

He knew he got a great deal because the dealer had told him.

At first I couldn't help sneering. Such a rube, I thought.

⇩

Despite the fact that I'm writing this book (or maybe it's because I'm writing this book) I look out at the world and the complex, fucked-up people who make it up and gasp at the vast improbability that two compatible souls can ever find each other, much less create a functional partnership.

Or maybe I've just had a run of bad luck.

All I'm saying is that if you get this far, you got a great deal. If you found someone who lights up your world, it doesn't matter what anybody else thinks. It doesn't matter that people shake their heads, wondering what you could possibly see in that person. All that matters is how you feel. That, and how you make that other person feel.

Rejoice in that. You done good.

But as I reflected on it, I realized that he was not just fine, but actually pretty goddamn brilliant. He could afford the truck, whatever it cost. And the money wasn't worth the frustration, the stress, even the effort.

He was happy.

And it made me envious.

I have a tendency to revisit the past, over and over again, wondering if I could have done better. When it comes to my profession, that's actually a good thing. I'm constantly improving. But when it comes to things I can't change, it's stupid. There was actually one point where I bought a car and figured that I'd paid too much for it. I never enjoyed driving that car.

The average homeowner stays in a house for more than 13 years. That's a long time.

In 13 years, what's your house going to be worth?

Well, you can't know. At least in terms of money. What you can know is that it's going to be your home. Do the best you can do and get the best help you can find and when the deal is done, move from shopping to owning.

Thirteen years from now, when you're thinking about moving into your next house, you're not going to remember that you could have done $3,000 better in the negotiations. That is, unless you beat yourself up over it for 13 years.

Enjoy your home. That's why you're buying one.

Rule #93
Moving Sucks

I. Hate. Moving.

Of all the reasons to buy a house, for me this is the biggest one.

If I never have to pack up my shit one more time, lose the stuff that matters, break the stuff that matters a little less, and not have room to put the stuff that doesn't matter but I can't figure out how to get rid of, I'll be happy.

Moving is expensive, frustrating, and painful. The older you get, the more painful it is.

Ugh.

Sleeping around is fun. Meeting someone, feeling that spark, burning fast and bright, and then moving onto the next one? That's kind of intoxicating.

For a while.

And then pretty quickly it becomes a drudgery.

Maybe it's because when you get older, your problems become more serious than where to spend your summer, but the thrill of always being with someone new is far outweighed by the desire to have a conversation about stuff that really matters: how to deal with aging parents, the loss of identity even when the career is going well, the state of the world.

Man, that sounds like it's all negative. It's not. There's also making plans for ten, twenty, thirty years out. Working together to give your kids the best education you can. Having a history together.

One of the most appealing things about being in a relationship

can also be one of the most frustrating: consistency.

But keep in mind that not having to move isn't the same thing as not being able to move. You can move. What's better, you can move with someone else. You can move together.

Moving by yourself, though. That means upheaval, expense, and uncertainty. And trust me, just like with moving from one house to another, it doesn't matter how careful you try to be, some of the stuff you care about the most is going to get broken.

Rule #94

If You Don't Fix It Before You Move In, You're Going to Live with It

When you buy a place, do two things: budget money to fix the things you want fixed, and don't move in until you get them done.

Not crazy about the color of the wall in the living room? Trust me, you're not going to like it any better when you get your furniture in there. But you're going to have one hell of a time scheduling a time to get to it and figuring out where you're going to put your furniture while you're painting.

You've spent your entire life becoming who you are and so has the person you're looking for. So when you meet, there's a pretty good chance you both have some stuff that the other isn't crazy about.

Maybe you like tossing your clean clothes onto the floor of the closet and your partner prefers to hang everything up. Or dishes. Your partner might not mind letting them pile up in the sink while you want them washed right away. Does the dog get to sleep on the bed?

There's a temptation to put up with stuff that bothers us, to not even bring it up. But you know what? Sometimes the person who's doing that thing that's kind of grating doesn't even care. You let it go and it's going to fester. Mark my words, when your relationship gets rough — and they all get rough — one bowl in the sink can set someone off and I'm speaking from experience here.

Bring it up. Make it a Festivus thing — the Airing of the Grievances. Do it now, while you're still getting along. When you still

⇩

Spouse Hunting: Using The Rules Of Real Estate To Find The Love Of Your Life

♥

like each other. When you're looking for ways to make each other happy.

Be honest about what bugs you and how much. And ask your partner to be honest back.

Then, when your relationship gets rough, you'll have to come up with other reasons to get pissed off.

Don't worry, you'll think of something.

Rule #95
You Get Out of Your Home What You Put Into It

The more you put into your home, the more you'll get out of it and I don't mean that as a spiritual thing, although it kinda is, and I don't mean money because you never make back what you spend on a place. It's really a practical thing.

Keep it maintained. Make it pretty. Address little issues before they become big issues.

Not only will your house make you happier, you'll get more out of it when it's time to sell.

The more you put into your relationship, the more you'll get out of it and I don't mean that as a spiritual thing, although it kinda is. It's really a practical thing.

Keep it maintained. Make it pretty. Address little issues before they become big issues.

Not only will your spouse make you happier, you'll get more out of them when it's time to sell.

Okay, forget that last bit.

Rule #96
Schedule Regular Maintenance

When I work with buyers, I keep a copy of the home inspection for the house they buy. Six months after they move in, I send it to them with a reminder to look it over.

Home inspectors find tons of flaws — that's what they get paid to do, so there's no way you're going to be able to address all of the things that "need" to be done. Six months in, you've kind of forgotten about the ones you didn't get to. But they never got done, did they?

I also recommend that you make a list of things that need to get done every year and set aside times to do them. Cleaning the gutters, servicing the furnace, painting the exterior. Put it in your digital calendar as an event that repeats annually. Then when it comes up, take care of it.

Then there are the monthly things. Checking the batteries in your smoke alarms, flipping your fire extinguishers upside down,

Like houses, relationships suffer when they're not maintained. So set aside a regular time to get together with the person you love and talk about things that are working and stuff that could be improved.

Don't forget the things that are working.

You got together for a reason. Lots of reasons. Remember those. Talk about those. Appreciate those. Then get into what you'd like to make better.

This isn't a time for personal attacks. And it isn't a time to say stuff like, "You never said anything about that before." You two are a team. So it's a time for you to work out how you're going to make stuff better together.

A therapist I know says you ought to schedule it once a month. That way you'll actually get to it once every other month.

It's not just this, though. Relationships, like houses, become our

cleaning out the fridge…

One of the worst things you can do to a house is nothing. It's called deferred maintenance and it kills a home's value more than anything short of a three-alarm fire.

day-to-day and when that happens it's easy to lose sight of what made them so special that we wanted to commit to them in the first place. So I think it's important for you to plan at least one vacation a year.

It doesn't have to be expensive — in fact, it's better if it isn't. The idea is to do something you both enjoy without having to deal with the daily routine and stresses. Going someplace you can't afford is a good way to turn a vacation into a reminder of the things that suck, and that's exactly the opposite of the point.

It's crucial to establish these patterns at the start of your relationship. Do them the first year and you'll have a much easier time doing them the second year. And a much easier time doing it the 20th year.

Oh, and one more thing. Just because you establish a minimum, that doesn't mean it should be the maximum. You don't have to wait for your scheduled check-in to talk. In fact, you shouldn't. Communication is so goddamn important to making a relationship work. Seriously.

Rule #97
You Never Really Own Your Home

If you remember one thing from this book, remember Rule #5, the one about making a list. That's important.

This rule, yeah, it's important. Not nearly as important as that other one, but still important.

And the point of this rule is that while legally, your home is your property, realistically it's a lot more. You are its steward. You have a responsibility to it and the more seriously you take that responsibility, the better your home will treat you.

I've talked a lot about people as property. It's important to keep in mind that I'm doing it to make a point, but that the point isn't that people are the equivalent of property.

The equivalence is in how you look for the partner. But the partner is as much a person as you are and should never, ever, ever, EVER be treated as anything less than you.

I know, in some cultures women are considered inferior.

We don't live in those cultures and if you do, what the hell are you doing reading this book?

You don't own the other person any more than another person owns you. So treat them like a human being. Give them the respect you'd give another person. Hell, give them the respect you'd want yourself.

And for god's sake, do something special on their birthday.

Rule #98
What If You've Made a Terrible Mistake?

If you've followed the steps in this book, it's super unlikely that you'll make a terrible mistake. Sure, some stuff won't be what you expect, but fundamentally you'll be living in a house that meets all of your needs and most of your wants.

But what happens if you aren't?

Get out.

Do it as quickly as possible. Take whatever loss you need to. Just go.

As you're doing it, think about the things that worked and the things that didn't. Especially the things that didn't. And figure out how to avoid making the same mistake again.

I was making dinner one night while my then-wife was flipping through channels in the living room. I made dinner just about every night, so it's not like I don't know my way around a kitchen. But this time it just wasn't coming together. The flavors weren't working. And the more I did to try and save it, the worse it got.

I finally took a break and went into the living room and sat down on the couch next to her.

"Are you happy?" she asked me.

"No," I replied.

"Me either. I want out."

I was talking about dinner. She was talking about our marriage.

That's how I found out I was getting divorced. Hell, that's how I found out we were having serious marital problems.

If I had to do it all over again, I would have moved out that night. I would have given her the house and all of my money. At the

Spouse Hunting: Using The Rules Of Real Estate To Find The Love Of Your Life

time, though, I thought I could have done something to save the marriage. I offered to go away with her. I offered to send her away by herself, anywhere she wanted to go. I tried to talk her into going to couple's therapy and when I finally did, I'm pretty sure she only agreed so she could get the therapist to tell me, "You need to be divorced." Which she did.

By the time it finally sank in that she had made up her mind and nothing I could do was going to change it, I had gone from being the person she no longer wanted to be in a relationship with to the person who was single-handedly responsible for every terrible thing that had happened to her.

She maxed out the home equity line of credit I had gotten on the house and used the money to hire a lawyer with a reputation for... let's say he accomplished stuff that more reasonable lawyers were reluctant to try. She got him to overturn the agreement we'd worked out. The one where I gave her the house and $110,000 I didn't have

⬇

and accepted all responsibility for our marital debt, but that we'd have shared custody and I'd get to be with my kids 50% of the time. Long story short, her lawyer turned out to be quite capable. I ended up giving her not just the house and 50% of the marital assets, but also 90% of what I had before I ever met her, half of my IRAs, and the pension I'd earned as a DGA director prior to ever meeting her. I was required to pay for her to hire a babysitter when she had the kids and then her lawyer worked it so that parenting time is pretty much what you'd get if you were a convicted felon or a child molester. (For the record, I'm neither.)

She even testified, under oath, that I was such a bad influence that it would be better for the children to be with the babysitter — a 24-year-old whose previous experience was working as a waitress and who had no training with special needs kids — than their own father.

I mention all this to make a point. The point is that it takes two people to be married and only one to be divorced.

Spouse Hunting: Using The Rules Of Real Estate To Find The Love Of Your Life

If it's over, it's over. Get out. Move on. The quicker you get out, the more likely it is that the two of you will remember the things you valued in each other to start with and if there are enough of those, you'll end up with if not a friendship, at least a cordial coexistence.

I have one of those, as I've mentioned before, a really close friendship with a woman I was as good as married to — someone whom I remember fondly in every phase of our lives together, from when we were friends to dating to living together to moving to three different cities together to splitting up amicably and choosing to live next door to each other so that the cats and the dog could go back and forth freely between our homes. I don't regret that we're no longer together — we both moved on — but I love her and respect her and am eternally grateful that she's in my life. So I know that it's possible.

My ex and I have been divorced now for almost nine years and I've healed from the scorched-earth legal campaign she waged. But we're not friends. We can't be.

Spouse Hunting: Using The Rules Of Real Estate To Find The Love Of Your Life

After all we'd been through, I can't remember a single good thing about her. A single good thing that isn't entirely superficial, that is. There must have been some. Hell, there must have been a lot. I chose to marry her at one point, so there must be a lot more to her than a big smile and a sense of humor.

That's sad.

Rule #99
Express Your Gratitude

You can express your gratitude to me by referring me to your friends, your family, in fact, anybody you know who's looking to buy or sell a home.

I'd certainly appreciate it. But that's not what I'm talking about here.

Appreciate your home. Take a moment every day to remember what it is that made you choose it over every other home out there.

It's tempting to see only the negative stuff. Don't do that.

You know that song "You Always Hurt the One You Love?"

So. Damn. True.

Don't take your partner for granted. Remind yourself every single day just how difficult it was to find that person. How hard you tried. How much you suffered. Remember the shitty dates, the smelly people, the situations you found yourself in when you thought you would never, ever find someone to walk through life with. Remember the jokes you told that didn't get a laugh, the dinners you ate where neither of you could think of a thing to say.

You did something super hard. And so did your partner.

Celebrate each other.

Brian Belefant is a licensed Oregon Broker in Portland, Oregon

You probably know him as Brian Your Favorite Realtor.

This book is more than a book. It's a gateway to resources. Go to SpouseHunting.net to tap in.

If you want to reach Brian, he's at (310) 854 2458 and BrianYourFavoriteRealtor@gmail.com.
On Facebook, he's @BrianYourFavoriteRealtor
On Instagram, he's @OldCarsOfPortland
And Milo (Best Puppy Ever™) is on Instagram as @MiloSpeaks, where he does occasional
commercials as Brian's official spokespuppy. For real.

Made in the USA
Middletown, DE
28 May 2022

66359404R00243